Gender and Identity Formation in Contemporary Mexican Literature

LATIN AMERICAN STUDIES
VOLUME 12
GARLAND REFERENCE LIBRARY OF THE HUMANITIES
VOLUME 2113

Latin American Studies

David William Foster, *Series Editor*

The Contemporary Praxis of the Fantastic
Borges and Cortázar
by Julio Rodríguez-Luis

Tropical Paths
Essays on Modern Brazilian Literature
edited by Randal Johnson

The Postmodern in Latin and Latino American Cultural Narratives
Collected Essays and Interviews
edited by Claudia Ferman

Readers and Labyrinths
Detective Fiction in Borges, Bustos Domecq, and Eco
by Jorge Hernández Martín

Magic Realism
Social Context and Discourse
by María-Elena Angulo

Resisting Boundaries
The Subject of Naturalism in Brazil
by Eva Paulino Bueno

Lesbian Voices from Latin America
Breaking Ground
by Elena M. Martínez

The Jewish Diaspora in Latin America
New Studies on History and Literature
edited by David Sheinin and Lois Baer Barr

Jewish Writers of Latin America
A Dictionary
edited by Darrell B. Lockhart

Readers and Writers in Cuba
A Social History of Print Culture, 1830s–1990s
by Pamela Maria Smorkaloff

Borges and the Politics of Form
by José Eduardo González

Voices of the Survivors
Testimony, Mourning, and Memory in Post-Dictatorship Argentina (1983–1995)
by Liria Evangelista
translated by Renzo Llorente

Gender and Identity Formation in Contemporary Mexican Literature
by Marina Pérez de Mendiola

Gender and Identity Formation in Contemporary Mexican Literature

Marina Pérez de Mendiola

Garland Publishing, Inc.
A member of the Taylor & Francis Group
New York and London
1998

Library of Congress Cataloging-in-Publication Data

Pérez de Mendiola, Marina, 1960–
Gender and identity formation in contemporary Mexican literature / by Marina Pérez de Mendiola.
p. cm. — (Garland reference library of the humanities ; v. 2113. Latin American studies ; v. 12)
Includes bibliographical references (p.).
ISBN 0-8153-3194-0 (alk. paper)
1. Mexican fiction—20th century—History and criticism. 2. Gender identity in literature. I. Title. II. Series: Garland reference library of the humanities ; vol. 2113. III. Series: Garland reference library of the humanities. Latin American studies ; vol. 12.
PQ7203.P46 1998
863—dc21 98-35873
CIP

Printed on acid-free, 250-year-life paper
Manufactured in the United States of America

CONTENTS

CONTENTS

Gender and Identity Formation in Contemporary Mexican Literature

PREFACE: MEXICO, AN OPEN BOOK

The five authors included in this book are part of the new outstanding generation of Mexican novelists. Miguel Barbachano Ponce, though a contemporary of Juan García Ponce, Carlos Fuentes, José Emilio Pacheco, Vicente Leñero, Elena Poniatowska and many other noted writers, does not figure here as an anachronism. By including him I hope, on the one hand, to close one of the lacunae in Mexican literary critical history. On the other hand, I wish to highlight the currency of his first novel for studies devoted to the analysis of different literary constructions of sexual, historical and social identities.

In the same way in which the generations of Salvador Novo, Octavio Paz, Rosario Castellanos, Carlos Fuentes, José Agustín, and Gustavo Sainz left indelible traces on the national culture, the generation of Blanco, Borbolla, Domecq, Roffiel, and Sefchovich is inscribed without a doubt on the new pages of the history of Mexican literature. Critic Ignacio Trejo Fuentes reminds us that "each generation tries to surpass that of the 'masters'." He adds that "one of the basic characteristics of the contemporary Mexican novel has among its purposes the shaking off, once and for all, of features imposed by prior examples, and the search for other distinct voices" (144). The voices of Blanco, Borbolla, Domecq, Roffiel, Sefchovich, and Barbachano Ponce have formed by breaking the prevailing authoritative norms of their predecessors and contemporaries. This does not mean, however, that their novelistic production lacks the literary qualities which historically characterize the work of "recognized" authors. The criteria of aesthetic quality are changing and not for the worse, as the keepers of a Modernism who seem to have forgotten their own premises would have us believe. By way of thematic and formal experimentation and through the quality of their prose, these authors give us proof of their active participation in the reorientation of Mexican cultural capital.

With this book I hope to show that these authors deserve to be known and studied. I invite other literary critics to devote new analyses to those segments of Mexican literature that have not yet been canonized but whose important literary contribution cannot be denied. Despite their newness in the literary landscape, these writers already have a considerable number of publications to their credit. José Joaquín Blanco, in addition to his literary work, also devotes himself to literary criticism and urban reportage. Among his works, one on Vasconcelos entitled *Se llamaba Vasconcelos* (1977) stands out, as well as his essays *Retratos con paisaje* (1980), *La literatura de la Nueva España* (1989) and his chronicles *Función de medianoche* (1981), *Cuando todas las Chamacas se pusieron medias de nylón* (1988) and *Un chavo bien helado* (1990). Brianda Domecq published her first novel, *Once días...y algo más* in 1979, and in 1982 she published a book of short stories *Bestiario doméstico*. Like Blanco and the majority of Mexican writers, Domecq ventures into literary criticism and essay. In 1987, *Voces y rostros del bravo* appeared and two years later she published *Acechando al unicornio*, an anthology of texts written in Mexico City, including texts on the theme of virginity. She has a new novel and another collection of essays in preparation. Sara Sefchovich also writes literary essays and in 1985 she published *Ideología y ficción en la obra de Luis Spota* and in 1987 *México, país de ideas, país de novelas: una sociología de la literatura mexicana*. In 1989 her anthology *Mujeres en espejo: narradoras latinoamericanas del siglo XX* appeared. Her first novel *Demasiado amor* was awarded the Premio Planeta for 1990 and was a best seller. Her second novel *La señora de los sueños*, published in 1993, was another best seller. Rosamaría Roffiel to date has published a book of poems *Corramos libres ahora* in 1986, a book of testimonies *Ay Nicaragua, nicaragüita!* in 1987, and she has a second novel in preparation. It should be mentioned that Roffiel began her career as a self-taught journalist and she worked more than ten years at *Excelsior*, three years at the magazine Proceso and four years at the magazine *fem*. Oscar de la Borbolla's books include four collections of short stories: *Los sótanos de Babel* (1986), *Las vocales malditas* (1988), *El amor es de clase* (1995), and *La ciencia imaginaria* (1996). He also published two humorous-erotic novels, *Nada es para tanto* (1991) and *Todo está permitido* (1994), and a collection of essays originally published for *Excélsior* since 1985, *Ucronías* (1990). Many of Borbolla's publications such as *Nada es para tanto* and *Ucronías* have been reprinted. In addition to the publications listed here, all the above mentioned writers still publish their essays in diverse periodical publications, cultural supplements, and reviews.

There is no doubt that this new generation is invigorating Mexican *fin de siècle* literature. In 1992 Mexico was honored by the central theme at one of the most prestigious book fairs, that of Frankfurt, under the title "Mexico an Open Book" (*Memoria de papel* 5, IV). With respect to this event, the President of the National Council for Arts and Culture, Rafael Tovar y de Teresa, declared: "Mexico is the first nation of Latin America to receive the distinction of being the central theme of the fair, which represents a unique opportunity to display a complete testimony not only of our history through the book, but also of the most important and current achievements of our culture" (*Memoria de papel* 5,

IV). As their inclusion at the Frankfurt book fair indicates, the novels that inspired this book are exercising a vital function in the realm of Mexican literature. May this study contribute to the dissemination of these novelists and help other critics to appreciate the contributions of this new literary generation.

This book would not have been written without the continous financial and intellectual support of the Center for Latin America at the University of Wisconsin, Milwaukee. The Center for Latin America's summer research grants allowed me to travel to Mexico with frequency and to access material invaluable to my research. I wish to thank in particular Iván Jaksic, director of the Center from 1989 to 1994. For his indefatigable work to keep Latin American studies alive during his tenure at UWM, I am deeply grateful. Howard Handelman for taking over the direction of the Center and for being a wonderful acting chair of the Department of Spanish and Portuguese during difficult times. Julie Kline and Cheryl Darmek for running the Center with efficiency, competence, and humor.

I wish to extend my gratitude to the Center for Twentieth Century Studies at the University of Wisconsin, Milwaukee, and, in particular, to associate director Carol Tennessen and director Kathleen Woodward. I thank Kathy for creating an especially conducive environment for the development of new ideas and dialogues during my fellowship year and the subsequent years I spent at UWM. The Center has, in many ways, helped me mature intellectually and professionally.

To Robin Pickering Iazzi for her abiding friendship and professional integrity. To Herbert Blau for his warmhearted moral and intellectual support; to Patrice Petro for fighting the right battles; Santiago Daydí-Tolson for believing in me and for his tremendous wit; to Julio Rodríguez-Luis for his optimism and intellectual energy, and for being a superb chair.

To David William Foster who entered my academic life when I most needed it. He read untiringly every page of the manuscript in its penultimate form, and played a vital role in the completion of the book. *Gender and Identity Formation in Contemporary Mexican Literature* is indebted to him in ways that exceed conventional academic acknowledgment.

My thanks and appreciation also go to the College of Letters and Science under the leadership of Dean William Halloran and Associate Dean Jessica Wirth for providing me with seed money to translate the manuscript into English. To Todd Burrell for his skillfull and prompt translation.

My gratitude also goes to Karen Stolley, Jaime Concha, Dalia Judovitz, Claire Fox, Andy Bush, Danny Anderson, Ksenia Bilbija, Guido Podestá, and Salvador Fernández who shared with me research ideas. Oscar de la Borbolla,

Beatriz Escalante, Miguel Barbachano Ponce, Brianda Domecq, Manuel Gutiérrez, Ana María Concha, Mima and Najib Fayad, and my students for their support while I was writing the manuscript.

To Ainhoa, my daughter, for delaying this publication and for allowing me to make it stronger. Finally, I would like to express my personal gratitude to Panivong Norindr for being a constant source of comfort, for making me happy, and for playing a vital role in every project I undertake.

Earlier versions of chapter III (in Spanish) and chapter IV (in English) have appeared in articles in *Inti* 39 (1994), and in *Bodies and Biases* (edited by David William Foster and Roberto Reis, Minneapolis: University of Minnesota Press, 1996). I am grateful for permission to reprint these sections.

CHAPTER 1: INTRODUCTION[1]

Mexico is known for its active and bustling literary life, in spite of the economic difficulties confronting the publishing world and the disillusionment displayed by some dissatisfied critics and writers.[2] For those who long for the heated, though clever and sometimes humorous polemics that once accompanied the appearance of new works, Mexico is one of the few nations that keeps the great literary arguments of old alive. Just reading literary reviews, watching television programs devoted to literature, or participating in conferences organized in Mexico City is sufficient to realize this fact. Moreover, the contemporary Mexican novel is one of the richest in the Hispanic American continent, both for its abundance and creativity and for its diversity. This diversity presupposes a divergence, a detour, a difference, and a digression, and it problematizes traditional chronological and thematic taxonomy, which leaves many critics, writers, publishers and especially literary historians, in a state of perplexity. Contemporary Mexican literature's resistance to traditional division into periods provokes an uncertainty that in the Mexican domain translates into a disillusion very characteristic of *fin de siècle* eras. Jorge Aguilar Mora speaks of

> a huge confusion in the Mexican novel, a lost sense of direction. It's like a crisis of narration in Mexico (among current narrators, myself included). There is no one with that grand sense of security to write a first sentence like *Pedro Páramo*'s: "I came to Comala because they told me my father lived here." There is no writer currently capable of anything like this. (Torres 133)

It is valid to ask here whether Rulfo himself, at the moment of writing the above

---

[1]All translations of quotes which appeared originally in Spanish or French are mine.

[2]For a history of publishing houses and literary production in Mexico, see Victor Ronquillo's excellent essay "Editores en México: Nace un libro" and Danny Anderson's articles "Cultural Studies and Reading Culture in 20th Century Mexico," and "Reading, Social Control, and the Mexican Soul in *Al filo del agua*."

sentence, experienced "that grand sense of security" which Aguilar Mora assumes. In any case, editors like Joaquín Díez-Canedo, of the Joaquín Mortiz publishing house, agree with Aguilar Mora. Díez-Canedo defines the literature of these last twenty years as "more a calling" than a "work." He adds:

> what is certain is that the future Pazes, the Fuentes, the Leñeros and the Poniatowskas are nowhere to be seen, the Pachecos, Sabines, Arreolas, Pitols, Elizondos, Galindos, Monterrosos, Garibays, López Páezes, and García Ponces, the Arredondos, Castellanos and Vicens of the 21st century. Perhaps their reincarnations are no longer possible today, nor necessary. (59–60)

The pages of the present study are devoted to a group of Mexican writers who do not form any part of the above mentioned canon, nor do they aspire to be "their reincarnations." These are: Miguel Barbachano Ponce, José Joaquín Blanco, Brianda Domecq, Rosamaría Roffiel, Sara Sefchovich, and Oscar de la Borbolla. The criteria for selection of novels in this study differ from those utilized by literary historians, and they do not follow the usual kind of thinking about what literature *is*. The "imperfect" novelistic body (as opposed to a regulating fiction and running counter to a society and culture based on a "moral unity") on which this study focuses does not lend itself to a rigid line of classification. These novels do not necessarily coincide in time; they tell very different stories and they are located in spaces not always contiguous. Nevertheless, the novels by Blanco, Barbachano Ponce, Domecq, Sefchovich, Roffiel, and Borbolla share characteristics that permit a subversive association, and my purpose is to make this association manifest. Said characteristics give rise to discursive practices which adopt changes in the way in which literature approaches notions as complex as history, sexuality, and identity. The five critical reflections proposed hereafter are centered around the literary, historical, and social development of characters in search of a redefinition of the sexual-gender system within which they find themselves imprisoned.

The basis of this work is rooted in the feminist deconstructionist and poststructuralist approach to texts and "in theorizing the construction of subjectivity" in novels which have not yet been the object of such study. The issue of which theoretical approach or models to use when analyzing Latin American literature is a sensitive one among Latin Americanists, a point I will develop shortly. The variety of theoretical tools on which I draw in this study helps to emphasize the fact that the political and the historical in Mexico are inextricably linked to the problematic of language and representation. Each of the following chapters was conceived to unveil different textual strategies these Mexican writers use in their works of fiction in order to dialogue with and ultimately transgress the sociopolitical and historical status quo circumscribing Mexican sexual and social identity formations. I believe that the study of the "contextual" and/or the "experiential" which ignores the literary articulations of these concepts sets up, as Homi Bhabha puts it, a "theory-practice polarity" (*Locations* 179). Furthermore, I would agree with Hannah Arendt and Bhabha, who convincingly argue that the "sign of the political is, moreover, not 'invested in the character of the story itself but only [in] the mode in which it came into existence.' So it is the realm of representation and the process of signification that constitutes the space of the political" *(Locations* 190).

Yet some readers might still object to what they could see as an insufficient contextualization in my readings of Mexican literature and for my "scrutinizing language" which, for many Latin Americanists, favors a theoretical inquiry of the semiotic networks at the expense of the content. I wish to take the opportunity here to clarify and define my position as an interpreter of Mexican literature and literature in general.

Context, Universalism, Historical Document

Sarah Webster Goodwin in her essay entitled "Comparative Literature, Feminism, and New Historicism," explains that for both historicists and feminists "historicizing the text means reading it in a context to which it is integrally related." History, she adds, "is not a back-drop, not something of inferior interest from which the text emerges in order to transcend it" (249). What is of particular interest in her assertion is the use of the verb "transcend" and the implied question of literature conceived as a discursive practice that "transcends culture."

The negative and pervasive association of the word literature and the verb transcend allows for a narrow understanding of the concept "transcending" and by extension of literature, an understanding that stresses the general to the detriment of the specific, sameness instead of difference. If we reconsider, however, the definition of the verb "transcend" as "going beyond the limits," we can think of literature as extending notably beyond ordinary limits. Literature understood as transcending culture would therefore not dismiss the material conditions in which it is produced, or underestimate the culture of which it speaks. Rather it is by going beyond the limits imposed by culture and material conditions that literature is able to fashion them, shape them, and reinvent them. I can only agree with Peter Brooks that "the contextualization of literature in ideological and cultural terms" needs "to remain aware of the use of poetics and rhetoric in understanding the way in which literature creates meaning" (103).

Moreover, a great number of Mexican writers, including several of those studied in this book, have expressed in one way or another their eagerness to be part of universal literature rather than seeing their work reduced to its national affiliation. This does not necessarelymean, as it is often reductively claimed, that they have internalized colonial patterns or become Mexican "Jacobins" and dismissed their Mexicanness. Those who advocate for a certain universalism, explains Susan Sniader Lanser, "have been committed not only intellectually but politically to the notion that literature and aesthetic culture are universal [...] focusing on problems that transcend linguistic and national boundaries." She adds, citing François Jost, that "the entire globe shares identical literary interests and pursues similar literary goals" (296), a position that emphasizes a "common humanity." These Mexican writers are themselves constituted in culture, yet it is a culture that is creolized. As Sniader Lanser points out "much of the globe including Europe—is becoming what Ulf Hannerz calls "creolized," so that even to speak of individual nations or continents, or "east" and "west," is becoming culturally incaccurate" (296). In his incisive essay on the issue of "Indigenism, Cultural Nationalism and the Problem of Universality," Neil Larsen draws on Samir Amin's 1989 work on *Eurocentrism* to explain that it is an

> impasse[3] reflecting the difficult historical conditions of emergence of the universal social and cultural project first given critical and scientific expression by Marx, that underlies the general intellectual distrust of universals. Insofar as postcolonial studies evinces this same distrust, it no doubt reacts to the dominant, Eurocentrist culturalism. But by the same token, it also reveals its objective incapacity to go beyond the bounds of cultural nationalism as apolitical practice. (134–35)

---

[3]Larsen glosses Amin's explanation for this impasse in the following manner: "Despite the incipient breaks with this Eurocentrist, or as Amin also terms it, economistic Marxism marked by the Russian and Chinese revolutions, the universalist project of Marxism suffers, because of its economistic distortions, a severe, if temporary, setback, leading to a so-called impasse in which there is a revival of Eurocentrist apologies for the "free-market" and Western liberal capitalism as genuine universals and a parallel resurgence of cultural nationalisms on the periphery, often taking the form of religious fundamentalisms, or what Amin refers to generally as "inverted Eurocentrisms" (134).

Furthermore, to consider literature as a national and historical document, as many critics in Latin American studies do when stressing the necessity to contextualize literature, prevents the literary text from transcending ordinary limits. A document is defined first as "an official paper" and second as "a writing conveying information." To document is defined first as "to furnish documentary evidence of," or "to construct, produce (as a movie or a novel) with high proportion of details closely reproducing authentic situations or events" (Webster). This equation of literature with the concept of evidence, of authentic reproduction, dismisses the very essence on which literature is founded; that is, its fictitiousness. Literature remains first and foremost a fictional product and cannot be reduced to a document. When approaching literature as fiction we need to ask not so much which contextual issues are thematically relevant, but rather how they are semiotically articulated, in which way they become mediated by literary language.

The problems related to the positioning of literature as document or fiction are best exemplified by approaches to the testimony. In 1994, I was invited to participate at a symposium on Rigoberta Menchú and to respond to John Beverly's paper entitled "The Real Thing" and to Elzbieta Sklodowska's paper "Wor(l)ds in Dispute: Afterthoughts on Testimonio and Rigoberta Menchú." In my response I took on the issue posited time and again in various essays already published and in their papers: the relationship between testimony and literature, or testimony as a new literary form.

In one of his essays Beverly urges us to read the *testimonio* not "against the grain" ("a contrepelo") or in a deconstructive manner, but rather "against literature," a formula which also serves as the title to one of his books. To read "against literature" means for Beverly "to question or to displace the role of literature as a hegemonic cultural institution"(x). In this debate on whether *testimonio* should be read as a literary text or against it, or outside of it, one of Beverly's main concerns remains the inherant dangers of this type of affiliation. Although he agrees with Edward Said that *testimonio* as literature should be seen as "another way of telling," or with Marie Louise Pratt that *testimonio* as literature could be seen as "a contact zone where previously disarticulated subject positions, social projects, and social energies may come together," Beverly still fears, and rightly so, that "even the most iconoclastic or progressive literature is simply forging the new forms of hegemony" (xiii). Yet one question remains (and it is by no means a new one): isn't revolution, in a Gramscian sense (and by extension *testimonio* as a struggle for liberation), a struggle for hegemony between opposing classes?

Testimonio, even as a new form of literary narrative, exposes itself to being read outside of what Beverly calls the "requirement of struggle for liberation and survival." However, despite the very real possibility of this type of decontextualization, I contend that testimony should *unquestionably* be read in literature, as a new form of literature, and therefore enter the realm of world literature with all the risks this type of coming together or assemblage entails for *testimonio*. By denying *testimonio* to be read in literature, we deny Menchú's testimony to participate in what Homi Bhabha and others, such as Eric Hobsbawm, call the "invention of tradition," a process which "estranges any immediate access to an originary identity or 'received' tradition" (*The Politics of Location* 2). Homi Bhabha further explains that

> the social articulation of difference, from the minority perspective, is a complex, on-going negotiation that seeks to authorize cultural hybridities that emerge in moments of historical transformation. The 'right' to signify from the periphery of authorized power and privilege does not depend on the persistence of tradition; it is resourced by the power of tradition to be reinscribed through the conditions of contingency and contradictoriness that attend upon the lives of those who are 'in the minority.' The recognition that tradition bestows is a partial form of identification. In restaging the past it introduces other, incommensurable cultural temporalitites into the invention of tradition. (*The Politics of Location* 2)

By participating in the invention of tradition, *testimonio* as a genre would not be standing outside of the process; rather, it would be creating it, therefore preventing its "domestication."

Studying Menchú's *testimonio* in literature allows us, for instance, to analyze how she appropriated us for her purpose, how she constructs this appropriation. When Menchú says "I am still keeping secrets nobody knows; not even anthropologists, or intellectuals, no matter how many books they have, can find out all our secrets" (1985: 247), I do not think that she wishes to inscribe herself exclusively outside of literature, nor to exclude as readers of her testimony intellectuals, critics, anthropologists, and so on. Rather, as someone who wished to become a Catholic catechist, by addressing us the way she does, she might be interpellating us not only in the Althusserian sense, but as Jesus Christ interpellated the Pharisees, "these men of letters," as Derrida puts it, "who he considered as blind, blind because they saw without seeing, with an eye that was too natural, too carnal, too external, which is to say too *literal*" (*Memoirs of a Blind* 18). As Christ, Menchú might be urging us, "blind Pharisees," "to clean inside the cup so that the outside also may become clean" (Gospel according to St Matthew 23: 15–17ff in *Memoirs* 18). In other words, it is a device that urges us to direct our eye toward the interior of ourselves in order to perceive that which she silences. She restores our sight by making herself partly "visible" so that we, in turn, participate in the process of shedding light on, or unveiling what remains to be told, because as Felman and Laub remind us that

> silence does not give peace. The "not telling" of the story serves as perpetuation of its tyranny. The events become more and more distorted in their silent retention . . . and pervasively invade and contaminate the survivor's and witness' daily life. (*Testimony* 79)

I believe Doris Sommer in her article entitled "Without Secrets" provided us with an insightful reading of *testimonio* as a new literary form. Sklodowska in her paper also built on this notion of secrecy in Menchú's text. She cautioned us against the danger of *seeing* "*testimonio* as a seamless monument of authenticity" which would subject Menchú to "suffocation or canibalization." She suggested that we take our cue from the voice of Menchú, reminding us that "testimonio's literary and political power ultimately stems from the witness's *Ethos* which remains unscathed by her sense of disorientation and discontinuity." I would agree with Elzbieta Sklodowska that Menchú's voice should also be heard through her secrets, through the incongruities between the real facts and what she narrated, or what Beverly calls her "literary inventions" (I am refering here to Menchú's narration of her brother's execution and the debate over the authenticity of the facts narrated).

As cultural and literary critics it is our responsibility to analyze how and why historical agency is transformed through the signifying process. This will reveal other dimensions of the text. For instance, Menchú is very much aware of what Felman and Laub define as the "historical imperative to bear witness," but she is also aware that "this imperative could essentially not be met during the actual occurrence" (Felman and Laub 85). Therefore, as a survivor, she engages in what Felman and Laub call the "act of testimony to also reclaim her position as a witness, reconstituting the possibility of a witness or a listener inside herself; in addition the act of testimony allows her to face a loss and mourn" (85).

I do not think that the heyday of *testimonio* as a narration of urgency is over. Urgency is where you wanted it to be. It is not over because Menchú's *testimonio*, this "trace of the real," can also be read as what Homi Bhabha calls an "unhomely fiction," a "fiction which would focus on those freak social and cultural displacements, as a fiction which relates the traumatic ambivalencies of a personal psychic history to the wider disjunction of political existence" (*The Politics of Location* 11–12). Such forms of social and psychic existence Bhabha adds, "can be best represented in that tenous survival of literary language itself, which allows memory to speak" (*The Politics of Location* 11). Reading *testimonio* as an "unhomely fiction" facilitates if not the reconciliation, the *rapprochement* between testimony and literature since as Bhabha optimistically argues

> when the present tense of testimony looses its power to arrest, then the displacements of memory and the indirections of art offer us the image of our psychic survival. To live in the unhomely world, to find its ambivalencies and ambiguities enacted in the house of fiction, or its sundering and splitting performed in the work of art, is also to affirm a profound desire for social solidarity: 'I am looking for the join. . . . I want to join . . . I want to join'. (*The Politics of Location* 18)

Theory, Latin American Literature and Elitism

The concept of joining brings me to the question of literary understanding and theory. By positing that literature can not simply be reduced to political, cultural, and economic contexts, as new historicists recommend, I am not advocating a return to formalist criticism. A middleground is necessary, and that explains why poststructuralist theory and deconstruction has informed my reading of contemporary Mexican literature. As Rey Chow reminds us the scrutiny of language was "one of the key pedagogical aims of poststructuralist theory [...] a theory which questions the logocentric bases of humanistic culture in the west" (114, 111). And yet, the question around the use of Western theory when reading non-Western texts remains a central preoccupation among many Latin Americanists as a recent call for papers for the 1997 MLA Convention attests: "Cannibalizing theory: submissions should explore the various implications of applying non-Latin American theoretical models—for example, those of Said, Bhabha, Spivak, and so on, to the study of Latin American literature and culture" (*MLA Newsletter*, Spring 1997: 12). Although my purpose here is not to engage fully in this debate, I would like, however, to contribute a few brief thoughts to it, developing upon a point presented by Rey Chow. She convincingly demonstrates that

> it is worth arguing that one of the strongest justifications for studying the non-West has to do precisely with the fundamental questioning of the limits of Western discourse which is characteristic of deconstruction

> and poststructural theory. The questioning of the sign as such leads logically to the opening up to the study of other signs and other systems of significations, other disciplines, other sexualities, other ethnicities, other cultures. (in Bernheimer 112)

By playing the devil's advocate one could contend, however, that this questioning of the limits of Western discourse is still carried out *within* and shaped by Western discourse. One thing remains nonetheless indisputable and it is that poststructuralism and deconstruction do not just provide a theoretical "model" one could apply indiscriminately. The word applying, in this case poststructuralist theory and deconstruction, is a misnomer and the idea of applying logically impossible since each discursive practice, whether literary or other, gives rise to different questions and different forms of questionings and forces us to define new ways of challenging them. The process of questioning can hardly be circumscribing, at least in theory. I believe that the central issue, however, is not so much the canibalization of theory, but rather the fact that the act of questioning is a privilege not within everyone's reach, which leads many to exclusion and alienation.

Living and thinking in relatively democratic countries and work environments gives me the opportunity not to apply poststructuralist theory, but to practice it. It will be recalled that the practice of theory within the West has itself been the object of sharp criticism and has generated many debates. One of the issues that directly concerns my work, since some of my readers have criticized me for it, is the much denounced question of theory's "esoteric terminology" or "jargon." Allow me to call on Wlad Godzich's brilliant response to this prevalent critique in our field of study. In his book *The Culture of Literacy*, Godzich reminds us that "the primary concern of theory has been more with the well-lit and dangerous zones where absolute knowledge is at its strongest under the species of unity and transparency" (26). He shows that to follow an "organization of knowledge ruled by a Hegelian inheritance" is to deny difference:

> The thought of difference tries to make audible all discourses rendered inaudible by Hegelianism, statism, patriarchism, hegemonism, totalitarianism, and so on. It attempts to render visible all the language that has been erased by the imperatives of transparency, thus becoming a labor of opacification, of restoring opacity where it has been glossed over. (26)

Yet as a student in one of my recent graduate seminars in comparative literature objected, opacity also implies exclusion, since one needs the tools to decipher it.

This brings us back to the equation of theory with elitism.

It seems to me that this equation is only a smokescreen that prevents us from addressing the core of the problem which is, first, the misuse of theory by many academics, and second the fact that access to a genuine mode of theorizing/questioning is often denied to most of our students and readers. The misuse of theory is carried out daily in many universities by colleagues who limit themselves to refering to theoretical movements without explaining them and who revel in words and concepts they often never define. This leads to an empty rhetoric which unfortunatly too often alienates the most open and devoted student and reader. By hiding behind what I call fraudulent opacity, an opacity far removed from the one Godzich advocates, we, as teachers, only usurp our power. Academics often fail to guide students/readers into the uncomfortable space of questioning language without which they will not be able to find "new ways to navigate the system whether it be academic, social, or political" (Godzich 28). Those of us who deny access to theory to our students/readers by malpracticing it, or by vilifying it, also keep them outside the process of "inventing tradition" and knowledge.

In this book I hope to show that literature and theory are, in fact, not such an odd couple. On the one hand, as I mentioned it earlier, literature is made of "unhomely moments": it is "a fictional evocation of in-betweeness," this liminal space that allows the critic to "get to new theoretical spaces;" on the other hand theory, as Godzich presents it, is "a philosophy of the cry, a cry constituted by difference in all of its avatars . . . a difference that cannot be contained in the unity that is presupposed by immediacy and beyond absorption" (26–27). If literature is made of ambiguous uncomfortable moments, of discontinuities, and silences that theory will "cry out" in multiple ways, shouldn't we see theory as the fictitous extension of literature, as another imaginary construction, as an "inevitable fiction?"

Practicum

Building on the work of historians, anthropologists, psychoanalysts, cultural, and literary critics, I hope to shed light on some of the new ways the five authors I study here have devised to address the issue of social, political, historical, and literary exclusion. However, every critical speculation in this book is also induced by feminist thinking. The feminist approach, as Teresa De Lauretis reminds us, does not suggest a debate or a set of single premises; rather it favors the theorization, through diverse discourses, of the literary construction of multiple characters. Each novel opens a critical space and I would hope to demonstrate through the present study that a feminist critical posture allows the posing of questions which are theoretically linked in multiple ways.[4] The idea of plurality is crucial here.

As Ana Lau Jaiven explains, "the women's liberation movement is no doubt joined to the general history of Mexico, where the image of the latter always appears inserted in the struggle to change the world around it" (23). In effect, since Sor Juana Inés de la Cruz during the colonial period, moving to Josefa Ortiz de Domínguez, Leona Vicario, and Gertrudis Bocanegra in the period from independence to the Mexican revolution, women performed important roles. This participation did not bring about the social, legal, or constitutional reforms needed to improve the situation of women in society. Nevertheless, the feminist chronology established by Lau Jaiven reveals that, decade after decade, feminist consciousness-raising efforts have gained ground. Certain dates stand out in particular. In 1906 a women's group, composed of Juarez supporters and professors of teaching colleges, demanded the right to vote. In 1913 María Arias Bernal organized the *Club Femenil Lealtad* and protested the death of Madero. In 1914 divorce was legalized and in 1916 Hermila Galindo edited *La mujer moderna* and requested the vote for women. The same year, the first Feminist Congress was organized in Yucatán, and in the states of Yucatán, Chiapas, and Tabasco women were given legal equal right to vote and be elected to public office by popular vote. In the Constitution of 1917 women's work was regulated and two years later the Mexican Feminist Council appeared and published *La mujer*. In 1935 the United Front for Women's Rights (FUPDM) was formed to seek the vote and the spread of literacy, child care, and maternity and other hospitals. Not until October 17, 1953, however, was Article 34 of the Constitution amended: women can vote and be elected in municipal, state, and federal elections. The National Union of Mexican Women was created in 1961 and nine years later what Lau Jaiven calls the "first wave" of feminism in Mexico emerged. The contributing factors to feminism's development in Mexico were first, the political protests in 1968 and the participation of women, mostly from universities, in political parties. In addition, the conferences and marches of North American feminists in the United States had a great impact on their Mexican peers. From 1971 until now several feminist movements have been organized, taking

---

[4]On the theoretical plurality included in feminist criticism, see Teresa de Lauretis's essay "The Technology of Gender" in *Technologies of Gender: Essays on Theory, Film, and Fiction* 1–30.

concrete form through the creation of leagues and associations: Women in Joint Action (1971), one of the first widespread associations, the National Women's Movement (MNM, 1974), the Mexican Feminist Movement (MFM, 1976), Feminist Struggle (1978), National Front for Struggle for Liberation and Women's Rights (FNALIDM, 1979).[5] In the eighties and nineties feminist movements also diversified and new programs were set up, such as, among others, Woman and the Environment, which extends to several nations of Central America and the Caribbean. Publications appeared, such as *fem*, a monthly feminist publication which, besides offering feminist articles on diverse topics, devotes two sections to spreading information relevant to social, feminist, or gay rights issues on the national level, for the Hispanic American continent and in the rest of the world. These sections were created with the idea of improving communication between feminists, gays, and other individuals in Mexico interested in the development of a feminist consciousness, as well as similar groups in other regions of the world.

Parallel to these feminist groups, and probably inspired and encouraged by their activities, gay militant groups were created in the sixties, such as Lesbos, Oikabeth; lesbian groups, such as Lambda, a co-sexual group, the Gay Front for Revolutionary Action (FHAR). The creation of gay activist groups such as Gay Liberation Pride Group (GOHL, 1982), mostly male, and the Lesbian Group Patlatonalli (1987) became in all likelihood one of the most remarkable phenomena, since their militancy emerged from the need to legitimate a sexual desire considered *contra natura* by the Christian moral system.[6]

Feminist literary criticism is not entirely different from ordinary feminist militancy, since both those groups which theorize feminism and those centered in praxis start from a common principle: "that feminism and its propositions will end up influencing sooner or later the process of shaping ideology" (Sefchovich 1983, 21). The urgency of the situation, particularly the economic situation, has led practical feminism to have more impact in Mexico to date. As was seen earlier, the participation of feminist groups in the revision and development of

---

[5]For a detailed study of the evolution of these movements, see the valuable work of Ana Lau Jaiven.

[6]See the study by Tede Matthews, "Bienvenidos a Jotolandia", in *Outlook: National Lesbian and Gay Quarterly* 15 (Winter 1992): 55–62; Joseph Carrier, "Gay and Liberation and Coming Out in Mexico," in Gilbert Herdt, ed., *Gay and Lesbian Youth* (1989).

new laws, their daily contact with communities which they seek to educate and defamiliarize after centuries of discriminatory social norms based on biological difference between the sexes, remains vital. I want to return, however, for a moment to the ideas of praxis and theory, two concepts which in the West often imply a binary opposition. Many Western nations consider theory to still be in its initial stages in Mexico. As Debra Castillo pointed out in the case of Mexican feminism's creativity, many of the women devoted to critical reflection, who, throughout the years, take up methodical and organized intellectual constructions of a synthetic and hypothetical nature, are often the same women who conceive, create, imagine and produce literary works (see *Talking Back*). These same women participate actively in the resolution of social and legal problems in different communities: they create journals, organize conferences, inform, and above all, educate. The feminist critic is, in most cases, a writer, a journalist, an essayist, a militant, an educator. A multitude of practices converges in these women. The ideas and critical reflections of Mexican women such as Castellanos, Poniatowska, Bradu, Sefchovich, Domecq, Galeana, Tomasa, to mention only a few (women who performed and continue to perform several of the above mentioned roles), are characterized by their plurality. However, in the domain of writing Mexican women have been able to reflect on the concept of desire and sexual pleasure.

Many Anglo critics have recently devoted studies to literature and artistic production by Mexican women. Among them, the precursory study by Jean Franco, *Plotting Women* (1988), stands out; recently translated into Spanish and published in Mexico, its purpose is "to constitute a common ground for a feminist understanding of Mexican culture" (xii). Franco's contribution is invaluable not only for its critical novelty and wealth of information, but also for the start which it gave to the field of feminist and cultural criticism in Mexico. Another excellent and challenging study is Debra Castillo's *Talking Back* (1992), with respect to the problem, alluded to earlier, of the theorization and practice of feminism in Mexico and other parts of Latin America. Claudia Schaefer's book *Textured Lives* (1992) helps to keep active the still limited critical corpus surrounding the cultural expression of Mexican women. The book demonstrates clearly how the theme of the female social, political, collective, private, and intimate body resounds in diverse literary instances, as well as its cultural emancipation.[7] Cynthia Steele, with her study *Politics, Gender and the Mexican Novel 1968-1988* (1992), also offers, with a wealth of information and details, an integral vision of the evolution of Mexican literature since 1968. Like Schaefer, Steele examines Mexican writers and artists "to explore narrative contradictions between political and social critique, on the one hand, and conceptions of gender roles and relations, on the other" (Steele 26).

In this study I hope to enter the debate and contribute to the dialogue which these critics have opened. Taking into account the fact that, generally, their studies are centered more in the "canon" of artistic production by both Mexican men and women (Kahlo, Poniatowska, Castellanos, Fernando del Paso, José Agustín.), I have chosen to devote this book to authors and works of lesser diffusion. This decision springs from the concern I have of seeing forgotten the creations of Mexican artists whose contribution to the cultural world of Mexico also deserves to be recognized and studied.

Beginning with the idea that a hermeneutical exercise should not be circumscribed by archaic and tribal essentialisms, I have decided to include in this work novels with characters of both sexes, written by male and female authors of all ages, diverse social classes, heterosexuals, homosexuals, and bisexuals, but all Mexican, of course.[8] As the five novels included here all combat the idea of the Mexican man or woman as a "unique subject," my purpose is to analyze the narrative strategies used by the authors to create multiple subjects.

The male authors here have not been included by "canonical custom." There is no doubt that despite the recent and healthy critical interest in narratives written by women, criticism of works written by male authors still prevails. Through the analysis of the five novels the fact that phallocentrism and the Law of the Father define and impose on us social, historical, and sexual identities, which also oppress men, will be remembered. What I intend to avoid at all cost, however, is the reproduction of the male/female gender and sexual binarism, the separatism that led us to hierarchies that today we seek to dismantle. I want to avoid falling into the trap of an oversimplified gender polarization. If, as critics

---

[7]Claudia Schaefer published *Danger Zone* (1996) as this book was going into press. I was, therefore, unable to dialogue and debate with her regarding novels such as *Amora* and the fictionalization of homosexuality and lesbianism in Mexico.

[8]I have left to one side important ethnic or racial dimensions, out of fear of including too much in a single work, which would result in not doing justice to any of the issues treated here.

reiterate fairly and frequently, the concept of the male and the female is not limited to a biological reality, then both "sexes" are victims of a system which, nevertheless, they help to build or maintain: the patriarchal economy. It is precisely the literary construction and deconstruction of these fixed identities which occupies the five novels of this study. These works offer us, as Hélène Cixous wrote, "another way of producing, of communicating, where each character is always more than one, where the power of identification puts the self to flight" ("Sorties: Out" 115).

The first novel analyzed here, *Demasiado amor* (Premio Agustín Yáñez for Novel 1990) by Sara Sefchovich, invites the reader to participate in the positing of consciousness, in the choices which Beatriz, the narrator, had to make in her life. *Demasiado amor* constitutes a brilliant example of what the exploration of one's subjectivity in the verbal and written world can include. The protagonist struggles to free herself from social and gender determinism that imprison her. Through the writing of texts, one epistolary and the other in the form of a personal diary, the narrator begins the search for a new self. This is only possible as long as the narrator first agrees to recall the seven years of her life that have just transpired. The act of writing allows her to perceive that, as Eugenio Donato explains:

> the identities and continuities generated by the repetitive mechanism of remembering, of reconstruction or representation, in reality hide an unresolved difference between the elements buried in the past of memory and the late recollection of the same in the present of representation. (576)

Hence the fact that, instead of avoiding the repetitive act of remembering, the narrator explodes the difference enclosed in such an act in order to create "an elaborate machinery of linguistic constructions and representations" (Donato 576) and to continue subverting the repetition and its representation until a new self is produced. I propose that this process of personal renewal is posited in Sefchovich's novel, both thematically and compositionally, in spatial terms. The reflections of French philosophers Henri Lefebvre and Gaston Bachelard on what constitutes space, its production, and its poetics, will provide the theoretical framework for the study of the narrator's social and sexual identity. How are the "practice of space or the perceived," "the representation of space or the imagined," and "the space of representation or the lived," articulated in Sefchovich's novel? And how do these diverse modes of thinking of space relate to the personal and narrative development of the protagonist-narrator? These are some of the questions to be posed in the first analysis.

The second chapter is devoted to the study of *La insólita historia de la Santa de Cabora* (1990) by Brianda Domecq, which transports us back in time to the nineteenth century. By locating her novel in an important historical period—that of the Porfiriato (the period of long rule by Porfirio Díaz, 1876–80, 1884–1911), Domecq follows the same path as many of her contemporaries and predecessors. In effect, Mexican literature is notable for its frequent use of history as a theme throughout. To verify this, a survey of the literary production of the twentieth century suffices. Behind the historicization of literature or the "literarization" of history is found the desire to rewrite that which was officially and scientifically documented in the annals of historical records. Driven by the need to defamiliarize the reader with official history, several novelists question not only the knowledge which scientific studies produced on the evolution of some past event, but also the methods which permitted the acquisition and transmittal of such knowledge. Of course, the Mexican agrarian revolution is one of the events which, decade after decade, constituted one of the inexhaustible sources for literary fictionalization of history.[9] Today, among the authors who renarrativize this period, women writers such as Silvia Molina, Angeles Mastretta, and Laura Esquivel stand out, with their respective novels *La familia vino del norte* (1987), *Arráncame la vida* (1985), and *Como agua para chocolate* (1989). These novelists, like their predecessors Rosario Castellanos, Nellie Campobello, and Elena Garro, whose literary footsteps they follow, offer us another vision of the revolution and its literarization. They write with a posture and a sensibility different from their contemporaries. First, the very participation of these writers in the narratological discourse expands the epistemological system, at the same time challenging it. The creation of characters who attempt to transcend historical and social conditioning, as well as the social-gender binarism on which said conditioning is largely based, gives rise to a revisionist fictionalization and language of the Revolution and its myths. At the center of the national literature are found other historical events such as the student movement of 1968 and the massacre of Tlatelolco.[10] In the same way, the presence of events going back to the

---

[9]Marta Portal's work *Proceso narrativo de la revolución mexicana* is still one of the best study on this fictionalization.

[10]As Matré points out, twenty-four novels, in addition to testimonial works, were written on this theme between 1968 and 1984. After 1984 two more were published: *Regina* (1988) by Antonio Velasco Piña, and *A la salud de la serpien-*

Conquest, the colonial period, and the nineteenth century independence period in the fiction of the last twenty years is interesting.[11] Contemporary literature, however, has devoted few pages to the Porfiriato. Even fewer are those novels which take up the task of rescuing from anonymity (both historical and narrative) those historical figures of the female sex. Furthermore, Franco reminds us that during the Porfiriato, "traditionally strong in times of war and civil strife, Mexican women were slow to challenge the domestication of women and often fearful of taking a step into areas where their decency would be put into question" (*Plotting* 93). Domecq investigates the life of a character whom history forgot for almost a century, that of Teresa de Urrea, reintroducing her as a "human body in history."[12] Teresa's novelized history allows the reader to make contact with one of the possible subjectivities of Teresa. Paradoxically, the fictionalization of her life is an attempt to redeem her from the unjust "fondling of myths" (an expression borrowed from Fabienne Bradu) in which the circumstances of her time held her captive. In this analysis, I will show that Domecq's representation fills in the lacunae of historical memory. This fact highlights the theoretical positioning perceived throughout this novel and leads to a rethinking of some of its questions. If, as Maurice Halbwachs points out, historical memory is nourished by "past events chosen, associated and classified according to necessity or

---

te (1991) by Gustavo Sainz. See Vicente Francisco Torres in "De la Onda a nuestros días" (141).

[11]Among the most resonant novels, *Terra Nostra* and *La campaña* by Carlos Fuentes, and *Noticias del imperio,* by Fernando del Paso, should be noted here. Recently the novels of Ignacio Solares, *Madero, el otro* and *La noche de ángeles, La lejanía del tesoro* by Paco Ignacio Taibo II, *El México de Egerton* by Mario Moya Palencio, and *El naufragio del mar amarillo* by Juan José Rodríguez, stand out. The period of the conquest is also reconstructed in the work of Herminio Martínez, *Diario maldito de Nuño de Guzmán, La ballesta de Dios* by Eugenio Partida, not to mention Eugenio Aguirre's *Gonzalo Guerrero* or Carmen Boullosa's *Llanto or Novelas imposibles*. See the article by Ignacio Trejo Fuentes, which provides a summary of the works mentioned here.

[12]Texas archeologist William Curry Holden spent many years studying the Yaqui people of the state of Sonora, Mexico. He was surprised by the recurrence of the Saint of Cabora or Teresa de Urrea in his research. He decided to examine this figure more closely, which led to his historical work, *Teresita* (1978).

rules," is it not then appropriate for us to resort to another kind of memory in order to recall that which by chance or misfortune was excluded from classification? What are the criteria which determine what belongs in Mexican history and how are these criteria identified? As in the other novels studied here, in *La insólita historia de la Santa de Cabora* the concept of identity is destabilized and at the same time revised, a concept which loses the rigidity imposed by the ideological structures of the Porfiriato. It will become clear that in Domecq's novel many of the codes and procedures created to individualize a person in society (marital status, affiliation, photography, ID cards), which allow the person to recognize himself or herself as an individual, appear to be fraudulent.

This leads us to pose new questions: in a society in which the Porfirista "dome" advocated order and scientific progress, what place could a healer woman have? What place could a woman like Teresa have in a society based on traditional theories or on institutions like the family, and which in addition used science and biological reasoning to support the theory of insurmountable physiological, intellectual, and social differentiation between the sexes?[13]

In the third chapter I examine *Las púberes canéforas* (1983) by José Joaquín Blanco. I demonstrate that this novel emphasizes the need to provide a discursive space for male characters whose sexual activities and whose lives in general have also been stigmatized[14] by what Carlos Monsiváis correctly defines

---

[13]See the series of articles written by Horacio Barreda and compiled by Lourdes Alvarado in *Revista positivista* 9 (1909), under the title "Estudios sobre el feminismo". Barreda was one of those who feared the dissemination of certain "popular theories" which advocated the equality of rights for both sexes. As Alvarado explains in her introduction, "Barreda proposes that in order for progress to become a reality the natural order must be respected. On this point and in perfect correspondence with his philosophical position he quotes Auguste Comte, who declared: 'Progress is nothing more than the development of order'"(19). If, according to Barreda, the natural order is proof that women are physically and intellectually inferior to men, feminist allegations have no currency and fail to follow the "positivist outline."

[14]During the last two decades a considerable number of theoretical studies have been produced in the United States and some on the Spanish American continent on the social and literary formation of sexual identities. I point out here some that were particularly useful to me in reflecting on the limitations of the prevailing identification processes: *Gender Trouble: Feminism and the Subversion of Identity* (1990) and *Bodies that Matter: On the Discursive Limits of Sex* (1993) by Judith Butler; *Plotting Women: Gender and Representation in Mexico*

as "familial, or governmental, or ecclesiastical authoritarianism" (175). Monsiváis's use in the above quote of the conjunction "or," denoting difference, separation between the idea of family, government, and church, should be substituted, however, by the conjunction "and." In effect, the five novels studied here posit without exception the intimate relation that these three institutions have maintained amongst themselves and the damage this alliance has caused. David William Foster, in his groundbreaking book *Gay and Lesbian Themes in Latin American Writing* (1991), discusses at great length the power of the collaborative triumvirate and its disastrous effects on the life of nonheterosexual Latin Americans. As he points out, the question of homosexuality in particular was as much a taboo subject for leftists as it was for the ideology of military tyrannies (see chapter five "The Sociopolitical Matrix"). *Las púberes canéforas*, due to its somewhat romanticized plot, could be read as, in Schaefer's words, a "homosexual utopian discourse." I would agree with both Foster (see pages 136–39) and Schaefer that many of the novels dealing with the issue of homosexuality adopt an "essentially utopian stance . . . (utopian because the social code demanding the censorship of certain forms of cultural production has not been simply wiped away by the cancellation of formal censorship") (Foster 132). As Foster adds, it also allows for the creation of "a world of redefined semantic dimensions" (138).

(1989) and "Apuntes sobre la crítica feminista y la literatura hispanoamericana" *Hispamérica* (1986) by Jean Franco; *Gay and Lesbian Themes in Latin American Writing* (1991) by David William Foster; *Talking Back: Toward a Latin American Feminist Literary Criticism* (1992) by Debra Castillo; *Señas particulares: Escritoras* (1987) by Fabienne Bradu; *Mujeres en espejo* (1983) by Sara Sefchovich; *Gay Ideas: Outing and Other Controversies* (1992) by Richard D. Mohr; *Gay and Lesbian Youth* (1989) by Gilbert Herdt; the articles by Sara Castro-Klarén, Carlos Monsiváis, and Josefina Ludmer in *La sarten por el mango* (1985) by Patricia Elena González and Eliana Ortega; *Essentially Speaking: Feminism, Nature, and Difference* (1989) by Diana Fuss; "Algunas reflexiones teóricas sobre la novela femenina" in *Hispamérica* (1981) and "La sombra de la escritura: hacia una teoría de la producción literaria de la mujer latinoamericana" by Lucía Guerra Cunningham in Hernán Vidal's *Cultural and Historical Grounding for Hispanic and Luso-Brazilian Feminist Literary Criticism* (1989); "Un diálogo entre femenistas hispanoamericanas" (1989) also in Vidal; *Between Men* (1985) and *Epistemology of the Closet* (1991) by Eve Sedgwick; *The Lesbian Body* (1975) by Monique Wittig; *Pleasure and Danger: Exploring Female Sexuality* (1984) edited by Carol Vance; *The Ideology of Conduct: Essays in Literature and the History of Sexuality* (1987) by Nancy Armstrong and Leonard Tennenhouse.

Though literary criticism has included Blanco's novel in the category of "gay" literature,[15] I seek to demonstrate that his characters reject any kind of categorization. On the one hand, I propose that the performative sexual acts of the characters no longer constitute the definitive sign of homosexuality (a condition in reality determined by the heterosexual economy; see Beaver 115). We will see that many male characters have sexual relationships with persons of the same sex for financial reasons and that prostitution becomes a means of support. The entrance of these characters into the world of prostitution could symbolize the urgent need to leave the secret world of the closet and to justify a sexual activity which in other contexts is condemned and more difficult to practice because of the lack of a partner. On the other hand, I prove that some of the characters see the sexual relationship which they have with other men as an extension of a very privileged social practice in Mexico: *cuatismo*, or the relationship between close drinking buddies. Might these be some of the many strategies which these characters resort to in order to alleviate homophobic pressure and to realize erotic desire? What are the implications of eroticization of a dialectic which nevertheless does not admit gratification of sexual desire or the satisfactions of sexual joy as such? *Las púberes canéforas*, through the interaction and conviviality of male characters from different generations, also points to the problem of the aging of the individual and to the struggle to continue as an attractive and active member of an urban economy of desire which only admits as its object replicas of classic Greek statuary. I will demonstrate that the exclusion of the "older" person from the libidinal structure reproduces ruling prejudices in heterosexual logic. I also affirm that this exclusion puts "at risk" a heterosexual social construction which has no space in the homosexual order: that construction which rests in comparing male aging with an honorable and erotically attractive maturity. *Las púberes canéforas* questions the male privilege of age,

---

[15]Manzor-Coates in her informative introduction to the recently published *Latin American Writers on Gay and Lesbian Themes. A Bio-Critical Sourcebook,* edited by David William Foster (1994), argues that in spite of the fact that "a politics of gay identity and the notion of a gay community, as they function in the US and in some parts of Europe, are not common or typical in most of Latin America . . . the word gay is practically commonplace in most of Latin America" (xvv). However, she also adds that the creation of categories such as the "internacionales" in Mexico when referring to "modern homosexuals who assume a gay identity," or the alteration of the spelling of the word gay in Spanish to guei, are "two of the many examples of this process of indigenization in the realm of sexuality" (xxvi–xxvii).

of which women are ritually deprived.

As a fourth example of the destabilization of the concept of social and sexual identity taking place in Mexican literature, I offer an analysis of *El diario de José Toledo*, by Miguel Barbachano Ponce. This chapter breaks with the idea of a chronological continuity. Why wait until the fourth chapter to begin the study of a novel whose subject is also homosexuality, but which precedes Blanco's novel by almost three decades? First, because Barbachano's novel challenges precisely the very idea of periodization alluded to earlier. During the time when Barbachano Ponce wrote *El diario*, his work was defined as an anachronism in the world of Mexican letters. Thematically, like Blanco, Barbachano Ponce approaches the problem not only of prescriptive heterosexuality but also that of the limits defining male homosexuality in Mexico. His novel unfolds, however, around a male homosexual character who, within the phallocentric economy, was denounced for his femininity. The construction of an effeminate male gay character earned Barbachano Ponce severe criticism from those who saw this femininity as a way of ridiculing male homosexuality or rather the "manliness" of the same. Although it cannot be denied that gays have been the object of a systematic cultural emasculation, Barbachano Ponce's novel poses the following questions: Does male essentialism, that is, the idea that male homosexuality can only be defined within the parameters of virility and around the law of the phallus, constitute the only way of imagining male homosexuality? Is the body and its exterior physical features the only "sexometer" capable of determining and measuring the libidinal currents of an individual? Freud himself had intuited that the question was not so simple: "A feminine mind, bound therefore to love a man, but unhappily attached to a masculine body; a masculine mind, irresistibly attracted by women, but alas! imprisoned in a feminine body" (Silverman, *Male Subjectivity* 357). The possibilities are multiple and obviously those highlighted by Freud are without a doubt those which pose the most problems to the rigid and repressive heterosexual epistemic regime.

The history which Barbachano Ponce presents is that of a character whose intimate psychic space is female, but whose male body is irresistibly attracted to men. Must a man who feels he is a woman reject himself as a man? Must a man who feels he is a man but who libidinally wants to feel he is a woman deny his desire and/or his body? The novels by Barbachano Ponce and Blanco transcend the notion of man and woman, and problematize the categories of male and female nearly to the point of removing authority from the link which society rushes to make between biological "naturalness" and the notions of gender, which results in the fixity of identity. I will demonstrate that Barbachano Ponce, in order to explicitly introduce the idea of various sexualities and identities coexisting in a single individual, as well as the dissonance which this idea provokes, resorted to avant-garde narrative strategies which could only be studied and embraced as such during a revisionist time like our own. The currency of Barbachano Ponce's novel is appreciated when one takes into account the fact that, even in societies like North America (comparatively one of the most open to the issue of homosexuality), one must wait until the eighties and nineties for critics like Judith Butler to begin the theorization of sexual ambivalence and its philosophical and cultural resignification.

I am very aware of the reactions that a feminist approach to Barbachano Ponce's and Blanco's novels might provoke. Nevertheless, *Las púberes canéforas* and *El diario de José Toledo* participate, in my opinion, like the other novels analyzed here, in the current feminist debates over identity, sexuality, power, desire. Besides, it seems urgent to pose in feminist terms some of the problems included in a homosexuality defined in patriarchal heterosexual terms. I don't pretend to have solutions, since, as Eve Sedgwick states, there is no "epistemological foundation" (*Epistemology of the Closet* 43) which allows me to do so. I can only pose questions that may possibly lead to other questions. What I hope to prove by choosing a feminist perspective is that without the seminal work of feminists in Mexico and other countries, the dialogue between texts like those of this study would not have been possible.

Mexican critic Ignacio Trejo Fuentes reminds us that "even though female homosexual literature emerges, after a long delay, in relationship to male gay narrative, it does so with a surprising vigor" (147). In the last decade many feminist lesbian writers have burst onto the scene of Mexican narrative, notably Rosamaría Roffiel with her novel *Amora*, to which I devote the last chapter of this book.[16] In *Amora*, Roffiel affirms the importance of novels which seek to transform consciousnesses with respect to the literary construction of diverse identities. This novel refuses to use abstraction to narrate a very concrete reality, and it rescues those who form part of that reality from oblivion. To effect this literary rescue of a segment of society, Roffiel manages to combine in her novel a wide range of literary techniques and genres such as, for example, autobiography, dialogue, philosophical debate, and so forth. Her novel is presented as a

[16]David William Foster indicates that Amora may be considered the first openly lesbian novel in Mexico. See *Gay and Lesbian Themes in Latin American Writing* (1991), especially pages 114–18 on Rosamaría Roffiel. See also the brief but interesting introduction to Roffiel by Schaefer in *Latin American Writers on Gay and Lesbian Themes* 382–85.

hybrid product breaking many of the laws which traditionally constitute the literary genres which the author uses. We will see, for example, that the autobiographical text not only acquires vitality here, thanks to individual and intimate experience, but that it also is nourished in large part by plurality, the multiplicity that forms such experience. In addition, I propose that the narrator enters an interrogatory dialogue on the concept of lesbianism and its relationship to heterosexuality, a dialogue which could initiate an awakening of consciousness and could lead the thinking word to circulate as a reflection, at the same time allowing her interlocutors to subject her to the same kind of questioning which she poses. I will also show that the heated, emotional, and even angry debates around the theme of amorous relationships between women, do not have the power to erase the affirmations found in the narration, nor to debunk the textual strategies which contribute to shape essentialisms that *Amora* hopes to question. In effect, I propose that in her attempt to undermine what Butler calls the "ideal or image of the coherent heterosexual ideal" (122), *Amora* replaces this ideal with another essentialism, that of the lesbian utopia.

In my last chapter I chose to focus on Oscar de la Borbolla's erotic-humorous novel *Todo está permitido* (Everything is Allowed, 1994) for several reasons. First, Borbolla's novel bestows on my work on gender much needed humor. At the same time it allows me to delve into another serious issue, concerning the question of eroticism, pornography, and representation. In David William Foster's and Roberto Reis's recent edited critical anthology *Bodies and Biases: Sexualities in Hispanic Cultures and Literatures* (1996), three essays contribute significantly to the understudied issue of pornography in Spanish and Latin American literature and culture. Foster's essay is of particular interest to me since he focuses on feminine pornography in Latin American literature, a pornography that is, as he postulates, "both a site for the examination of the dynamics of patriarchal violence and the possibility for constructing an erotics that reimages relations of sexual power" (247). One could hardly call Borbolla a feminist, as he did not set out to write a feminist book per se. Yet his novel poses fundamental questions that have first and foremost been addressed by feminists, but also by men interested in feminism such as Stephen Heath: Are pornography and eroticism "anything more than a relation between men, which has nothing to do with a relation to women except by a process of phallic conversion that sets them as the terms of male exchange?" (Heath 2); "are pornographic images for male arousal necessarily the reproduction of domination?" (formulated in 1987 by Heath in a piece entitled "Male Feminism"). Borbolla's novel takes Heath's question further and asks: are pornographic images and texts only for male arousal?

In this chapter I hope to show that Borbolla marks a milestone in Mexican literature in the sense that he writes a seemingly pornographic novel with a male narrator, seemingly about "men together" and their fantasies, while simultaneously undermining the foundation that gives support to this kind of pornographic discourse. Borbolla is not a "feminist" yet he seems to be, as Heath puts it in his attempt to define men's relation to feminism, "writing or talking or acting in response to feminism" (9). If as Heath asserts "feminism makes things unsafe for men, unsettles assumed positions, undoes given identies" (6), *Todo está permitido* is probably one of the most unsafe novels of all the novels studied here. It is unsafe not only for men but for women as well, due to the accumulation of familiar cliches that crop up throughout the narration but also because in the mind of the informed reader, the story transforms, from a hilarious and buoyant erotic narration into a meditation and a critique on men's and women's sexual, social, and economic relations. This novel represents anything but stability and I hope to demonstrate that Borbolla walks a fine thin line between perversity and bonhomie, chauvinism and feminism, comedy and epistemology, a fine line that constantly threatens to break.

Each of the novels analyzed here stands out because of the theoretical questions posed on the very complex concept of literary construction of social, sexual and historical identities. Their authors do not ignore the fact that going beyond the notion of power represents, as Butler explains, "a cultural impossibility and a politically impracticable dream" (30), and therefore they use literature in order to rethink "subversive possibilities for sexuality and identity within the terms of power itself" (30). The proliferation of identities and sexualities which takes shape in these novels has the function of avoiding precisely "that one continue to think of the question of identity and of sexuality as something rigid and immutable which defines one from birth to death" (Butler, *Gender Trouble* 32). The literary texts included in this study represent only a sample of the "flood of novels" in which the problem of identity, of sexual difference and the discursive practices this generates, is inscribed. Therefore, many novels are yet to be analyzed in feminist terms. I hope, however, that the analyses provided hereafter will help to improve understanding the process of resemanticization of the notions of gender, sexuality and identity in contemporary Mexican literature, and that they assist and support other investigators.

CHAPTER 2: *DEMASIADO AMOR*: CARTOGRAPHY OF AN IDENTITY

Reading *Demasiado amor* implies the difficult deciphering of a novel in which diverse "textures" abound, textures that coexist, contradict, and exclude to the point of supplementing one another. Not only thematic and structural but also semiotic and stylistic richness force the critic to enter a leafy "garden of forking paths" that join again and cross one another, a space of convergences and divergences. The plot develops around Beatriz (whose name is revealed only on the last page of the novel) and her sister, two Mexican women whose parents have just died; they are about to fulfill their dream of acquiring a boarding house on the Italian Mediterranean coast. Lacking sufficient funds to pay the expenses for a trip for both sisters to Italy, Beatriz's sister makes the voyage alone, leaving Beatriz in Mexico's Distrito Federal in the apartment the two had shared with their parents. Beatriz's goal is to earn money, on the one hand, to pay for her sister's stay in Italy while she looks for a boarding house to rent, and on the other, to finance her own trip to Italy to join her sister.

Abrupt loneliness leads Beatriz to leave her apartment each evening to go to Vips, (a restaurant chain in Mexico) to drink coffee and meet people. Slowly, she eventually meets "men" with whom she agrees to go to bed so as "not to feel so alone" (41). This routine becomes a "profession" when her one-night stands leave money. Discovering that she earns more money going to bed with her conquests than she does in her boring secretarial job, she decides to have sex for money in addition to her regular job in order to send more money to her sister, and to save, as soon as possible, what she needs for her own trip to Italy. Among the men she meets at Vips, "the weekend man" is of particular interest; she falls passionately in love with him and she devotes all her weekends during seven years to him, meanwhile abandoning her dream of going to Italy. From a structural viewpoint, *Demasiado amor* is divided into two narrative sequences which unfold in parallel and alternating fashion as the narration advances to finally converge in the last pages of the novel. The most clearly defined and recognizable narrative sequence is that identified with the epistolary genre. In effect, part of the novel is composed of letters which Beatriz writes and sends to her sister in Italy. Each letter specifies the day and month in which it was written but not the year. The letters trace, linearly and temporally, the "history" of the two sisters—though more particularly that of the narrator/author of the letters—and the history of their dream.

The sister's answers to Beatriz's letters are not included as a text per se in the body of the novel. The sister's voice is filtered through that of Beatriz, and the reader only has access to the sister's responses by means of the commentary that Beatriz makes in her letters on what her sister has written. For example:

> November 4
> Hi, sis:
> What do you mean you're going to live in the house so you don't have to pay the hotel anymore? It must be a horrible mess there, with the workmen, the dust, the building materials! (35)
>
> November 29
> Dear sis:
> Listen, I'm very grateful to this Don Tito of yours. I'll even take him as a brother-in-law! What do you mean he wouldn't accept repayment of the loan he gave you? All the work I had to do to earn it! And what do you mean, he says he did it out of love for you? One of these times he really will love you. At least the help he has given you is good. Tell him thanks from me, and well, keep that money for savings if something comes up or use it to buy china. (135)

To a certain extent, Beatriz's letters include those sent by her sister. The epistolary portion of *Demasiado amor* functions as an explicative narrative and it advances the plot information. In these letters, Beatriz's routine is presented, and to a lesser extent that of her sister; the satellite characters, such as Beatriz's "clients," also appear in it. The letters allow us to see the evolution of the sisters' dream and their development as individuals. The narrative time is the present, as each letter supposes a periodic writing describing recent events sharing information and sentiments of the moment.

The second narrative sequence resembles a personal diary. It is constituted as a retrospective approach and it relates, mostly in past tense, the seven years of madness and passion that Beatriz lived with the weekend man. In this narrative sequence we also find passages written in the present, which Beatriz addresses to a "tú." This second person form of address assumes the presence of a reader in the form of the weekend man. "I remember when you had the urge to try every dish ever invented in this country. . . . Do you remember how many hours you kept me in the tub full of warm water so I'd be nice and soft inside. . . ?" (8, 20).

In the pages that follow, I propose an analysis of the function of these narrative sequences in Sefchovich's novel and their relation to each other. First, I wish to explore some of the ingredients that make up the diary or the text of the personal and private life of Beatriz, that which is unspoken, censured in the epistolary interchange. Second, I will approach the epistolary narration in order to define how the public persona of Beatriz is constituted. Said analysis will allow me to demonstrate subsequently the convergence operating between the two narrative sequences and the implications of this convergence for Beatriz's subjective formation.

From the "Representation of Space" to the "Space of Representation"

In the plural and polyvalent ocean formed by these two narrative sequences, the most significant thing, perhaps, is the preponderant position occupied by the idea of space and the role that the spatial dimension plays in the narrator's formative process. Let us see first how the notion of space is articulated in the diary.

The originality of this narration rests primarily on the fact that the narrator refers to her amorous relationship—an otherwise complete relationship—with the weekend man as if it were a long trip through the Mexican nation. In the same fashion in which the weekend man saves Beatriz from her loneliness and routine, taking her throughout the national space, the narrator invites the reader to penetrate and travel retrospectively with her through the multiple Mexican geographies which the weekend man is showing her. Suddenly we find ourselves nearly overcome with the river of words and proper names expounding the physical, cosmographic, botanical, zoological, historical, musical, political, linguistic, gastronomic, theological, mythological, and geological geography of Mexico. Initially we follow the weekend man from one place to another, as did Beatriz, behind him, "behind you and with you, following you, hearing you, seeing you, admiring you. . . . Because you showed me this country. You took me out and brought me back, you ascended and descended me, you introduced me to it" (20, 24). The repetition and succession of verbs whose exclusive subject is the weekend man points to Beatriz's passive receptor function expressed through the direct and indirect object pronouns "me." In the same way that passion dominated and took control of Beatriz, we are intoxicated and impregnated by the onomastic flood unleashed like an avalanche racing through the pages of the book. Nevertheless, as I observed earlier, the narrator's text is a reflexive one that attempts to understand the factors that contributed to the failure of a love that seemed to be indestructible.

In various places in the narration, Beatriz equates her love life with the idea of loss of identity and of will. By way of analepsis she attempts to undertake the long and difficult crossing that will lead to the recovery of her self: "I don't remember anything, I've forgotten everything, everything" (29). The second voyage, this time mental and commemorative, leads her to approach critically and suspiciously the space belonging to the weekend man, the space he showed her. The process of Beatriz's seduction by the weekend man develops without any difficulty: she feels abandoned by her sister, overwhelmed by an immense melancholy, devalued and willing to follow and fall in love with anyone who appears to be interested in her. The weekend man has at his disposal a woman who is young and eager to learn about love, life and the world. The role which the weekend man assigns himself, that of uncontested instructor of a young woman who has everything yet to discover, is one of the most widely generalized and most penetrating fantasies of the patriarchal world.

The weekend man does not teach, rather he instructs, imposing his vision of the Mexican national space, of love, and of eroticism. Beatriz perceives this only after seven years in the relationship: "And then I began to hate you. . . . I hated you, for because of you I forgot my dreams. . . . I hated you because of so many churches, so many hotels, so many parks, landscapes, suns, rains, nights, markets, gardens, roads. . . . But above all I hated you because you never asked anything about me" (171–72). At the end of the seven years Beatriz realizes that the space in which the weekend man moves and in which he caged her, is very different from the space in which she longs to live. The narrator presents the space of the weekend man as an imagined space, penetrated with a single knowledge, a space with which he identifies through the power that this same knowledge carries within itself and from which she is excluded. This type of space is what Henri Lefebvre more appropriately characterizes as a "representation of space."[1] The representation of space corresponds, in his opinion, to a specialized space, in search of stability, a space always capable of being explained, rationalized, homogeneous (61). The weekend man's space is a theoretical one, a space represented and ruled by specialties that only experts could decipher. The spaces (historical, geographical, ethnographic, gastronomical.) that he presents to Beatriz seem created and defined by specialists, discarding the possibility of seeing them transformed by users. The representation of the weekend man's

---

[1]I follow here the terminology defining and questioning the notion of space from the work of the French philosopher Henri Lefebvre in *La Production de l'espace.*

space operates as a strictly controlled totality. The process of critical remembrance allows the narrator to probe the only realm offered to her. Without a doubt the weekend man's imagined and determined space is not for this any less significant. Yet, to whom are his messages directed? If the representation of space is presented thus—"reality as a means of accumulation" (Lefebvre 152)—to what reality does it refer? Beatriz traverses the different levels (historical, social, topographical. . .) of the national territory but that does not mean that it includes her. As Lefebvre reminds us, that which is visible is not necessarily legible (100). The "modernist trio: visibility, legibility, intelligibility" to which Lefebvre refers ironically, here displays its fallibility, given that intelligibility is possible only for him who possesses the necessary codes for deciphering the visible. Beatriz is invited only to accept, to welcome, and to confirm the representation of space. The weekend man does not award her the privilege of decoding her space. According to Lefebvre's definitions of the representation of space, it seems safe to postulate that the weekend man functions allegorically as an "absolute political space, a strategic space . . . which seeks to impose as reality that which is nothing more than an abstraction, though one endowed with enormous powers by representing the place and means of Power" (113).

The passive verb form used in this narration emphasizes the peripheral role that Beatriz plays as she traverses the weekend man's domain: she is a mere user of a controlled space, the production of which she does not participate in. The weekend man could be read as a synecdoche of the Mexican national space defined by the nation-state, a space that implies a certain reading and prevents others, such as an oppositional reading. The space which the weekend man defines is sectarian, repressive, isolating, and rejecting the active participation in the process of its creation of whom the nation-state and the Law of the Father continue to exclude: woman as subject and integral part of the society. The Mexican nation-state never conceded the same privileges to women as to men, a fact which limits the access of women to the resources of men.[2] The weekend man replicates the system in force, assuring himself that Beatriz depends on him as a man and holder of power, "subsuming" Beatriz and women in general in the national body politic in a symbolic fashion. This spatial panorama is a simulacrum which deceives the "ordinary practitioner" of space (De Certeau 93).

On the other hand, anamnesis leads Beatriz to recreate part of her past, that is, to reconstruct piece by piece those moments lived with the weekend man

---

[2]See the important studies collected in *Nationalisms and Sexualities*, edited by Parker, Russo, Sommer and Yaeger.

and to create a past perceived in a mode of renewal. She does not restrict herself to remembering the weekend man or the representation of space that only molded her as raw material and changed her into an object so that she would fit perfectly in the national space. Rather, she desires to leave herself as object (which she refuses to be) and she addresses herself to that activity that produced her, in order to explain and shed light on the operations and manipulations that modified her, making her an object.[3] The narrator proposes instead to demythologize the "divine power" of the representation of space which the weekend man symbolizes, and the totalizing and deceiving fiction that said representation creates. By way of writing she offers us another space, the "space of representation." This permits us to enter into a dialectical relationship with the central nucleus of knowledge which corresponds to the representation of space or the weekend man (Lefebvre 134) and, in addition, to show that the representation of space is not operational without the space of representation which she symbolizes through her writing (Lefebvre 52–54). According to Lefebvre the space of representation "does not impose coherence or cohesion, and refers more to that which is lived than to that which is imagined" (52). It is a space that is "lived", "spoken", a space with a "nucleus or affective center which contains, comprises places of passion and of action" (52).

The weekend man's conception of space allows her to traverse and circulate in said space but prohibits her from imprinting herself upon it or marking it. She will achieve inscription on the surface texture only when she conforms with the type of inscription assigned to her. The weekend man would prefer to keep her in this "monumental space" through which he guides Beatriz. By definition, monumental space, Lefebvre explains, "offers to each member of a society the image of his belonging and of his social countenance, a collective mirror more real than an individualized mirror" (253). Nevertheless, Lefebvre also adds that the "use" of monumental space "does not provide all the answers immediately upon crossing its threshold" (254). The narrator questions the monumental space and shows that it does not always make for consensus. By way of her writing she, if not destroys, at least demythologizes said monumentality, refusing to let it become the only "metaphorical and metaphysical support of the society" (Lefebvre 259). She refuses to allow the "text" to be written for her and without her. In the space of representation constituted by the written text of her analytical memory, the narrator begins by marking out a territory thus distancing herself from the conventional tourist for whom spaces are already produced. She

---

[3]See Lefebvre on the concept of production of objects (133–35).

becomes a traveller, moving counter to the simulated order and to the total unity of the space.

As I observed at the beginning of this analysis, the flood of words in the narrative (the function of which is to trace as completely as possible an official map of that which defines and grounds the Mexican national territory), is capable of confusing, disorienting, and enchanting the most cautious of readers. One is carried away by the frenetic rhythm and the abundance of this national glossary. This flood of words presents itself as the nomenclature of Mexicanness. It seems as though the narrator is testing us, so that we can better understand the process of seduction which, as a woman enamored, led her to succumb to temptation. Soon, however, she helps us to disassemble the fraudulent mechanism which the weekend man used to carry out his seduction. She questions the simultaneous coherency of the lexical composition that represents the nomenclature of this national dictionary. She appropriates the system that subjugated her and uses to her own advantage the inflationary quality of this description to subvert "national knowledge," the weekend man's knowledge which is clearly shaped in said description. Therefore, the description carries out three functions in this text: the first is of a narrative order, since, as we saw, the description covers more than a paragraph in the text and is not merely a "fragment" of the corpus. The description partakes of the very time of the story line, forming a body to the point of invading the field of the story line in its totality. Its second function is that of suggesting how the national space or the representation is constructed, how it is ordered and hierarchized, how it is manipulated to achieve the unconditional adhesion of its users. The third function of the description as one of the narrative modalities of *Demasiado amor* is that of denouncing the epistemology of a limited number of "specialists" who base themselves on a determined and accepted knowledge, thus excluding the possibility of other knowledges. In this case, the very descriptions themselves serve to critique what Lefebvre defined as "a descriptive knowledge that withdraws when facing the analytical" (144). The description, in fact, places in doubt the manner in which the weekend man presents the national state to Beatriz, that is, as "a long and uninterrupted chain" (Bartra, in Cajas Castro 13). In this third function, the description as a mode of reproduction is exacerbated until, paradoxically, it no longer constitutes a means of representation or of signification, but rather a means of destruction of one's being or of the evoked object. The manner in which the narrator uses the description is very similar to that of the French "nouveaux romanciers" of the fifties and sixties. Alain Robbe-Grillet, one of the French novelists of this period, describes the function of "modern" description as follows:

> Description that once intended to reproduce a pre-existing reality now affirms its creative function. That description which used to make us see things now appears to destroy them, as though its zeal for discoursing on such things aimed only to confuse and blur its lines, so that they were incomprehensible, so that they disappear completely. (159)

Beatriz describes her past relationship and the sentiments that still arouse her love for the weekend man as a "double movement of creation and erasure" (Robbe-Grillet 160), of acceptance and of judgement. On the one hand she has not succeeded in ridding herself of the love she feels for the weekend man and, by extension, for the Mexico to which he introduced her. But on the other hand, she is aware that what he and the nation-state offer her as a woman is a slow death, a chronic and acute pain, a total abnegation of her being as a citizen, as a thinking, feeling, and desiring individual. To express this sentiment, the narrator uses the lyrics of the famous bolero entitled "Nosotros":

> No es falta de cariño, te quiero con el alma, te juro que te adoro y en nombre de este amor y *por mi bien* te digo adiós (179; emphasis mine)
>
> (It's not for lack of love, I love you with all my heart, I swear that I adore you, and in the name of love and *for my own good* I say goodbye).

Her descriptions contribute to the questioning of the intelligibility of the world, a world accessible to the woman willing to sacrifice everything, with the condition that she follow the rules imposed by the patriarchal ideology.

Therefore, the narrator not only uses description as a narrative mode to delineate the ideology that sustained her and to which she submitted out of love; she also uses it to euphemerize the ideology. She resorts to the same code of signification, to the same tropes, in order to reconstruct her experience as a woman and an individual, an experience that said code of signification omitted. She does not propose to separate her experience from that of the weekend man. On the contrary, she hopes to give proof that both experiences, that of her lover and her own, could coexist if the weekend man were willing to admit the existence and materiality of the woman that not only travels with him, but who constructs the voyage with him, who traces the lines on the map as much as he does. For Beatriz to admit that the weekend man "constructs his sexual gender within the patriarchal system with the goal of serving the interests of male supremacy" *(Making a Differance* 3) is a gradual and painful process. Her instinct for survival, however, both physical and mental, triumphs over her cutting pain. With her narration, she gains access to what was denied her, to what Roland Barthes defines as "access to the superior status of creation" *(Mythologies* 50). She refuses to shrink, the way a sharkskin seeks to satisfy the desires and passions of the man who uses it, but which shrinks each time it is used. Unlike the representation of space that appeals to a totalizing description, Beatriz's space, the space of representation, invites description which is contradictory, repetitive, bifurcating, and accumulative. She protects description which is "overburdened, self-negating, displacing in such a way that the very images question themselves as they are constructed" (Robbe-Grillet 160). By refusing to admit fixed images, she fosters ambivalence at the same time that she endeavors to understand how difficult it is to live fully in the name of her love. While Beatriz surrenders body and soul to her relationship, the weekend man lives his relationship with the narrator as would be expected of a typically macho Mexican male: he demands sacrifice, total surrender, and above all, her silence, forcing her to penetrate his secrets, to confront his reality: "Today my love story has ended, and with it all the meaning of my life. From now on, I'm going to disappear, to lose myself in the shadows, to let myself be carried away in easy, joyous loves, which are the only ones that do no harm, that don't hurt" (184).

From a feminist point of view, the narrator can only with great difficulty continue to accept a love that ignores and silences her power of creation, a love unable to hear what it refuses to understand. At the same time she knows that eroticism is "the imbalance to which the very being submits itself and through which it consciously places itself in judgement" (Bataille 37). In a way, as Georges Bataille explains, "being loses itself objectively" (37). Beatriz knows that there is no eroticism "if nothing overwhelms us in spite of ourselves, something which, no matter the cost, should not be, if we fail to achieve the senseless moment to which we extend every trance, and to which, simultaneously, we reject every trance" (Bataille 296). This aspect of the novel poses a problem to which feminist criticism will continue to give much attention. We are reminded that the relationships between feminism and sex are not yet resolved. Gayle Rubin, in her essay "Thinking About Sex" (an essay written more than ten years ago but in my judgement still one of the most influential works in the arena of North American feminist criticism), examines the limits that certain feminists impose on woman's sexuality. The relationship between feminism and sex is complex, Rubin reminds us, "because sex is the nexus of relationships between sexual genders and a large part of the oppression of women is confirmed in, mediated through, and constituted within sexuality" (300–301). This does not imply, however, Rubin continues, that the only escape for women, the only way to protect oneself from oppression is to close oneself to sexual pleasure, avoid erotic behavior, uncontrolled hedonism: "this type of pseudo-feminism recreates", according to her, "an arch-conservative sexual morality" (302). Without eroticism there is no life, even though erotic activity may be linked closely or loosely with death. Georges Bataille defines eroticism as "the approbation of life until death" (17). The fact that pleasure and desire always carry within themselves danger and transgression, therefore, does not mean that woman as an individual should be prevented from expressing and living her sexual fantasies. What matters is that erotic play should bring pleasure, and that the woman as a desiring individual participate in it and "control" the game to the same extent as her male partner (this is an issue taken up in the last chapter of this book). In fact, at the moment in which Beatriz fails to find satisfaction and even feels cheated, the choice is hers, and she finds the strength to turn her relationship with the weekend man into a memory which she alone controls, transcribes, and rewrites according to what she chooses to recall.

The space of representation recreated by writing allows the narrator to travel through memory nomadically, deterritorializing it to later reterritorialize a territory through which she moved as a tourist only. By deterritorialization, Gilles Deleuze and Félix Guattari understand a displacement, an exile of the "familiar" that allows one to begin the search for one's own identity in order to reevaluate "the stable place of origin" (Kaplan 191) that shaped one's self. For the narrator, it is not a question of remaining perpetually "outside" of the territory. Deleuze and Guattari point out that deterritorialization necessarily implies a desire for reterritorialization. From the locus of memory, Beatriz distances herself from the map that was traced for her. She distances herself from the mode of representing and apprehending space that has come to constitute itself as the only valid and legitimate mode, and which is based in a conceptual, rational, methodical, and systematic knowledge. She explores other more empirical paths which the national and patriarchal episteme circumnavigates and skirts to the point of crossing them off the map out of fear of the unknown, fear of what its codes and its science still refuse to recognize: sensorial space.

> Because you took me out and brought me back, ascended and descended me, you taught me and told me everything about this country, my country.
> And I heard it all, saw it all, I smelled it, tasted it, touched it. (33)

The difference between the two ways of living the amorous relationship is shaped in the indentation that separates textually and visually these two modalities. The narrator is not professing with this construction the incompatibility of the two modalities. Rather, she points out the peripheral position which the weekend man assigns to others' experiences or to any experience which his epistemological list does not include, thus denying the possibility of complementarity to which she aspires.

For Beatriz, space is not understood in a single, unified fashion, rather, she leads us instead toward a multiple decodification of that which surrounds her. She presents us with a different "code of knowing" at the same time as she approaches space also as an "extension of the body" (Lefebvre 238). She restores sensorial space as a stratum, a sediment which, as Lefebvre puts it, "persists in sedimentation, in the interpenetration of social spaces" (244) but to which no value is conceded. She emphasizes the "inventive capacity of the body." The presence of water and the sea in the narrator's text takes on great importance, being one of the privileged elements to which she resorts to make manifest said inventive capacity. According to Lefebvre,

> the inventive capacity of the body does not display itself: the body itself displays it, unfolds it in space. The multiple rhythms interpenetrate each other. In the body and its surroundings, as on the surface of water, as in the mass of a fluid, rhythms cross and intercross, superimpose one another, bound to space. They leave nothing outside them, neither the elemental pulses, nor the energies distributed in the interior of the body or on its surface, whether normal or excessive, the replica of an external action or explosive. (236)

The narrator refuses to submit her body to a controlled linear determinism. By including the tactile, the olfactory, and the other sensory functions, she goes against the Judeo-Christian tradition that ignores and despises the body, hides it and limits its functions in public. The objection could be raised that the very link established between the sensory, the corporeal, and female sexual gender goes against the idea of deterritorialization, since the patriarchal economy based, and continues to base, its ideology on this type of junction: woman/body-senses versus man/intelligence-reasoning. Nevertheless, what the narrator attempts to undermine is not so much the equation woman/body-senses, but rather the negativity associated culturally with this equation as well as the segregationist aspect that it implies. She hopes to transcend the sacred opposition between the imagined, on the one hand, and the lived, the perceived, on the other. With her text, she reestablishes equilibrium between words, language, discourse of thought, self-awareness, and sensory knowledge. She creates in this way a mixed space, and she redefines the conditions of entry in the exclusionist world of epistemology.

Thus she begins the process of reterritorialization and her inscription as an active and constitutive element in the collectivity. The text signals other strategies which the narrator employs to achieve this process. In effect, one of the "territorial" signs that she resorts to is that of repetition, which Deleuze and Guattari call the refrain, whose role as a territorial connection has been emphasized frequently (312). Scattered through the text in cyclical fashion we find a series of phrases repeated: "I remember," "because you showed me this country," "I think I've forgotten everything," "I don't remember anything," "I did it all," "you remember?" "you took me," you bought me," "the car stops, we get out," and so forth. These repetitions, many of them anaphoric, highlight the obsessive character of the relationship. They also function, however, paradoxically as a refrain whose effect is "sedative, stabilizing against the threat of chaos" (Deleuze and Guattari 311). The refrain allows the narrator to confront her recollection once the vertigo of memory is opened, to mark her territory, to put her signature to it with her presence. The refrain has the peculiarity of gathering, accumulating and joining forces in the heart of the territory, or it allows one to wait until one is able to leave the territory. These refrains, Deleuze and Guattari clarify, are "refrains of confrontation, of departure that at times bring a movement of absolute deterritorialization" (327). Hence the two notions, deterritorialization and reterritorialization, are inextricable from each other. The act of deterritorializing leads the narrator to a territorialization which then leads to a reterritorializing to begin again the deterritorialization. Like a travelling nomad, the narrator "divides and regroups, struggles or laments, attacks or suffers" (Deleuze and Guattari 341).

The inscription of the refrain in the space of representation allows Beatriz to transcend the place and posture that the weekend man assigns her through his representation of space, which is that of another object in the encyclopedic vignette, subdued and classified. She hopes to avoid "encyclopedic nomenclature" (Barthes 94) which, as Roland Barthes explains in *Le Degré zéro,* also "is based on the idea of possession", of "appropriation" (94): "the vignette not only has an existential function, but also, one might say, an epic function; it carries out the function of representing the glorious end of a long trajectory, that of matter, transformed, sublimated by man, through a series of episodes and stations" (98). The refrain allows the narrator to resume her genesis, her essence, her praxis.

In psychoanalytic terms we could say that the diary—the space of representation—supports and encourages repetition. According to psychoanalyst Ferenczi," in order to overcome the compulsion to repeat and at last make recollection possible", the act of repetition is beneficial and prevents the compulsion from becoming a pathogenic problem (Laplanche and Pontalis 8). The narrator-protagonist uses repetition, in plot as well as in composition, to force herself to remember. Likewise, the act of remembering, no matter how painful, sets in motion "the mechanism of detachment" which allows "the subject to free himself from repetition and from his alienating identifications" (Laplanche and Pontalis 487).[4] The narrator, through the space of representation, manages to recreate her obsessive relationship, in order to free herself from it and from her past.

Epistolary Topography, Spatial Reorganization, or the Desire for Space

The presence of space also plays an important role in the second narrative sequence—the letters which Beatriz writes to her sister. While the diary refers to the construction of the personal subject and Beatriz's life during the weekends, the letters inform us principally of the routine and the sentiments of the narrator during the week, as well as the evolution of her relationship with her sister. She does not write about the weekend man in great detail. She only mentions the great passion she feels for him.

Beatriz resents the fact that her sister has gone on alone, leaving her in Mexico with the responsibility of earning the money they lack to rent the boarding house in Italy. She writes: "meanwhile you live in a hotel and stroll by the sea. The truth is it makes me very angry. It's more than that, I'm furious" (19). The epistolary interchange between the sister and Beatriz is very regular during the first months of the separation. Certainly, the weight of loneliness, separation, and Beatriz's disillusion is a dominant factor in this. She can only imagine the things her sister is now discovering, feeling, and living. After the initial shock, with the passage of time, each sister on her own grows accustomed to the separation and reconciles herself to her new life. In the initial moments the boarding house, as the epicenter of the dream they share, keeps them close. Nevertheless, with time, not only distance separates them but also lifestyle. We perceive, as the epistolary relation progresses, that the dream, though it continues to be the same for both sisters, is being pursued by diametrically opposite means. This produces a most unexpected reversion: Beatriz's sister, who in the beginning characterizes

---

[4]In Laplanche and Pontalis, on the language of psychoanalysis, see in particular the definitions given of repetition compulsion (78) and mechanism of detachment (486–88).

adventure, risk, freedom, and the unknown, with her trip to Italy, becomes the epitome of traditionalism. Inversely, Beatriz, who, remaining in Mexico represents the habitual, the familiar, the ordinary, regular, common, and the ritual, is the one who now openly contradicts strict moral and social norms. While the sister takes root in Italy, Beatriz's life is changing radically.

Let us now examine the power that the narrator's public life has over the creation of her new identity. From the beginning of *Demasiado amor,* Beatriz's transgressive desires are made manifest. A large part of the fascination that travel holds for the two sisters emanates from the desire for flight, the desire to obtain an unconstrained space. The repeated allusions to the sea and to water, both in the letters and in the personal diary, is certainly indicative of the urgency that Beatriz feels to traverse unknown latitudes. Nevertheless, condemned to remain alone in the place of origin from which she hopes to flee (Mexico), Beatriz reorganizes her life so as to tolerate the melancholy that overtakes her and to speed her departure for Italy. As the novel progresses, Beatriz would appear to carry out fantasies that even she did not suspect could be hers. Most significantly, she fulfills them in Mexico, the place in which it seemed impossible to live out an adventure.

The first few occasions in which Beatriz goes to bed with her conquests from the Vips for money, she does so "to get out of a fix" (45). In fact, since she sends all her earnings to her sister to fix up the house in Italy, Beatriz is often without money to pay her own rent. Her sister sends her more and more onerous budgets, which forces Beatriz to earn more money, because she wants to keep her dream alive. In the end she finds herself trapped in a vicious circle: "Here I am, trying to get ahead. Listen, do you really need so much money? Your last letter shocked me, so no more stories; when I don't have enough even for my own expenses or to send you what you ask for, I'm going down to Vips to look for someone to invite to the house" (48). Nevertheless, Beatriz gradually grows accustomed to her new work, to the point of turning it into a lucrative business.

The above serves as preparatory information for a full entry into the analysis of the transformation process through which Beatriz passes, a process that takes shape in the spatial reorganization of her surroundings, the importance of which is crucial both in plot and composition in the narrative whole. Let us see first how this reorganization of space is manifested from the plot perspective.

The midpoint of Sefchovich's novel marks a fundamental plot twist, a twist that also affects the novel's structure. From that moment on, as we move through the reading of the letters, an almost "hyperbatic" transmutation is seen in the roles played by the sisters. The sister who leaves her environment for Italy, "abandoning" her family, breaking the familial bond to which Beatriz is so rooted, suddenly is transformed into a matron. She weds Tito ("a man more your grandfather than your father" (91)) and she has three children. As the family grows there is no longer room to take in boarders and little by little the house is settled domestically, becoming a place which in some measure is closed to the public. From explorer and businesswoman, open to change, the sister changes into a "good" wife who follows the precepts of the established order. She imposes her moral standard, a false and constrictive standard, on Beatriz: in reality the sister becomes a procuress, and moreover a moralizing one, demanding on the one hand that Beatriz turn over her profits, though stained by her illicit labors, while on the other hand easing her own conscience by denouncing and criticizing the very occupation that sustains her. She exploits her sister by way of the dream that they shared at the beginning of their adventure, at the same time gradually excluding her from that very dream. The boarding house that Beatriz paid for with great difficulty is turned away from its original function. The sister's dwelling by the sea becomes that of another person (Señora Genovesa), who even comes to occupy the position of Mother for the sister, appropriating the only space in which Beatriz hoped to locate her privacy, her future dreams. Finally, Beatriz's sister replaces her not only with another family, but with another provider, Tito, who from now on will support her.

As I have already observed, by remaining in Mexico, her environment of origin, the narrator limits herself to "a domestic flight." Surprisingly, the voyage that she takes turns out to be much more transgressive than the "international" trip of her sister. As the months pass, Beatriz changes her physical appearance: she cuts her hair, dresses less traditionally, and she becomes in fact attractive. The theft of Beatriz's graduation medallion almost a year after her sister's departure, a medallion "full of memories" (67), also takes part of her past. The relationship, in the final account a pleasurable one, which she maintains with her clients allows her to project her desire in an atmosphere totally alien to that prescribed by the established order. While her sister follows morally exemplary behavior, marrying and procreating, Beatriz subverts the idea of familial cohesion with her "act" and points to the possibility of happiness outside the traditional domestic sphere. In essence, she leads us to rethink, rather than to reject, the concept of family and domestic felicity. She does not glorify prostitution per se, rather she locates her desire and her sexuality outside of normative practice. She takes control of her body and begins an "ideological reappropriation of the body" (Monsiváis, *El nuevo arte de amar* 175). She writes to her sister: "Sometimes I think I like this work, that I'm not doing it just for the money, why deny it" (166). She gives free rein to her libido, to her sexual desire in search of satisfaction. This excess of satisfaction displayed by the narrator is opposed to the notion of "honor as the foundation of familial prestige" (Monsiváis, *El nuevo arte* 167). She questions one of the governing principles defining the family. Honor for Beatriz is no longer regulated and disciplinary; it implies instead self-respect and not a moral imposition that feeds into censure and silencing of her social and sexual identity. In this respect, the narration attempts to avoid the word "prostitution" and when it is uttered it is by the sister, who plays the role of "assuring the sanctity of the home." Likewise, a new Beatriz emerges gradually in her own country, echoing the "fundamental statements with which Mexican feminists have penetrated public opinion and civil society, achieving notable success" (Monsiváis, *El nuevo arte* 175). Beatriz writes: "I learned to ask for what I want" (120). The narrator's transformation in this narrative sequence is accompanied yet again by the reorganization of space and, more precisely, of the spatial order that her apartment represents.

According to Gaston Bachelard's argument in *La Poétique de l'espace,* home is the privileged place of dreaming, of a happy childhood, and this "image is transformed into the topography of our intimate being" (19). Home is equivalent to the idea of refuge, of consolation, and "it happily shelters the unconscious" (29). For Beatriz, however, the home that her dreams are building is not the home of a concrete recollection, but rather the home that only the future can create: the boarding house in Italy. In fact, "her house," the apartment, just as her parents and her sister left it to her, does not symbolize the space of peace to which she aspires. This explains why she first launches into a radical cleaning of the apartment and redistribution of its furnishings (36, 46). To the extent that she realizes that her "Italian" dream is vanishing, she finds herself in need of rethinking the space which her apartment in Mexico constitutes as a possible location for her dream. Her house gradually becomes a public place, a place where her clients are transformed into boarders. In addition, she opens the house to a gay architect friend who, in passing, decorates the apartment with all the amenities of a boarding house: new sofas, new bath towels, new bedsheets and robes, a mini-bar, and "even a servant who comes in twice a week to clean up" (132). Progressively the space and its redistribution become a game: the narrator rents the neighboring apartment and knocks out the wall between for more room, and she gets rid of the family furniture "to open up the space" (175). While the house in Italy is filled with mechanical gestures, the children and furnishings that traditionally represent domestic tranquility, the narrator's house becomes a "minimalist" space that tends towards neutrality and the simplification of forms and colors surrounding her: "There's not a stick of furniture, I threw it all out, not a single decorative piece, I gave it all away. I left the walls empty, the rooms empty, and the windows without curtains. . . . I've already taken out all the doors, too, and all the glass from the windows" (180–81). She reorganizes the spatial order and demolishes everything that limits and blocks "the open space." She is the one who chooses the "spatial signifiers" (De Certeau 98) which will carry out a transformative function. As Beatriz rethinks her space, the Italian dream recedes until relegated to a postscript in her letters. In the first letters written to the sister, everything revolves around the boarding house, and questions about the sister's life in Italy abound. In the last letters, however, Beatriz devotes more space to telling her sister of her own daily life, as her interest in, and preoccupation with, Italy diminishes.

"I'm two persons"?

Beatriz's catharsis takes form, as we have seen, in a narrative of auto-analysis which passes through recollection and memory. This examination, however, this retrospective view and the text that materializes it are supplemented by the narrative body of the letters:

> I'll never be the same again, because I live only in expectation of the weekends. I'm two persons now, one that works and one that flies, one that exists on earth from Monday to Thursday and another that settles into paradise from Friday to Sunday. (54)

"I'm two persons," Beatriz writes to her sister. Which is the person of the diary? and which is the person of the letters? Who is the person who lives from Monday to Thursday? Is she very different from the one that lives from Friday to Sunday? What can be affirmed is that neither of these two persons would be identified as the person that writes the first seven letters. In order to explain the bond that links these two persons and the two narrative sequences, we must probe the symbolisms common to both texts.

The Vips restaurant as a public space carries out an important function in both plot and composition. The glass doors of the Vips take on a magic hue. They represent access to another world. By crossing the threshold of the glass doors, Beatriz finds herself projected into a restorative space in which she begins her rebirth. The Vips comes to represent a vital space of harmonization in her life, the place that allows her to link her life from Monday to Thursday to that from Friday to Sunday (she meets the weekend man at Vips). The restaurant is a meeting place that joins her intimate personal life to her public and working life. In the same fashion, the Vips ratifies the bond between the two narrative sequences and functions as symbolic terrain which empowers the fusion of two apparently dissimilar texts. It could be read as a plot requirement. Significantly, the Vips represents the transitory space in which the two parts of a schizophrenic identity in full reconstruction are reunited, at the same time making manifest the opening that separates the two narrative utterances. In the passage in which Beatriz presents herself as two persons, "one that works and one that flies", discord, the detachment of a certain reality from a part of Beatriz, and the urgent necessity of keeping the public and private spheres separate are made evident. The *Spaltung*[5] or doubling that Beatriz experiences is more a symptom than a pathological condition. The presence of several distinct literary genres, even though very closely related, within a single novel, is a structural signal as important as the thematic signal that the Vips represents. In effect, the letters, which correspond to the epistolary genre, and the personal diary,[6] share various characteristics, both thematic and expressive: both texts display an awakening of consciousness, a self-examination in order to find a new meaning to life. Both resort, in different ways, to the "confessional" mode. In the diary, Beatriz needs to confess herself, in the sense of recognizing and exploring, to begin the process of self-analysis. In the letters, Beatriz reveals to her sister the tenor of her relationships with the men she meets in the Vips, in addition to details of her personal life with the weekend man. In neither of the two narrations does the narrator flee from her emotions, and both modes of expression manifest her desires for action.

On the hero of the confessional novel, Peter Axthelm points out that the "craving for action is so extreme that he would accept even the most painful act" (17) and in the case of Beatriz, I would add, the most risky. What shines through clearly in both narrations is the compulsive nature of her actions. In her diary this takes the form of profuse description and repetitions, as well as in the idea

---

[5]For a psychoanalytic definition of schizophrenia, see Laplanche and Pontalis.

[6]Martens, in her work on the morphology of the diary, reminds us that beginning in the twentieth century writing a diary does not necessarily imply a daily, chronological writing. "Contemporary definitions like that of the *Dictionnaire du français vivant* show that the diary is no longer thought of as a strictly quotidian record. The emphasis on regular writing has been dropped . . . ; the temporality implicit in the etymology of the word no longer plays any part in its meaning, for the diarist does not necessarily describe the events of each day, nor does he describe daily" (29–30). The personal tale of Beatriz can be defined as a diary in the sense that it documents—although retrospectively—past events of her life with the weekend man.

of her obsessive love; in the letters it is manifested in the thematic repetition of her relationships with different clients. Like the Gogolian or Dostoievskian hero, Beatriz longs to live deeds that would "provide some fuel for [her] romantic dream of conquering" the world that surrounds her, "excruciatingly aware of [her] impotence and [her] position" (Axthelm 19).

Consequently, by way of this series of common denominators, Beatriz is very aware that her *Spaltung* is a symptom of a malady which she must remedy. In a way, she attempts to blur the boundaries between two narrative subjects and their respective experiences between the private and the public, to create a proper space for the reconstruction of an identity based on a equilibrium between the external and the internal.

In the last pages of *Demasiado amor* the two narrative sequences fuse to form a single narration. In the same way that both spaces of representation (that of the diary and that of the letters) are linked, we can observe the conjunction between spaces which geometry traditionally separates: the "inside" space and the "outside" space. Bachelard would have considered that these multiple spaces which Beatriz creates and inhabits, her inside and outside spaces, "interchange their respective vertigo" to the point of "exasperating the boundary between the two" (*La Poétique* 198). The narrator describes this fusion between the external and internal as follows:

> The house is like a park, with plants, balloons, butterflies, a dark brown carpet. My friend Gómez turned the bathtub into a fountain full of fish. (180)

> The light comes in through the bare windows: intense in the morning, brilliant in the afternoon, timid at dawn, determined at midday, strange before dawn. The darkness enters, the gray of some days or the yellow of others. You can feel the wind, the heat, the humidity, the cold. . . . Butterflies fly everywhere and you can hear the chirping from the many cages of birds. (181)

On the function of the window, French critic Jean Rousset reminds us that for Flaubertian characters ("characters at the same time immobile and adrift"), the window occupies a privileged place: "In a closed place where the soul gathers mildew, the window symbolizes a tear through which one diffuses into space without having to leave their point of fixation" (441). In the case of the narrator, not only her being "diffuses" into external space thanks to the window; rather the totality of the house and its interior unfolds and opens. The house fills with breath and finds itself "at the limit of reality and irreality": at times, Bachelard indicates, "the house of the future is more solid, brighter, roomier than all the houses of the past" *(La Poétique* 68). It is no longer the house where she was born, nor is it the boarding house in Italy. The narrator's house is a space restored by a true "dialectic between inside/outside," a dialectic that insists on "intimacy," which represents and is shared by the inside and the outside, "always ready to invert, to interchange their respective hostility. . . . It represents a mixture between being and nothingness. . . . The intimate space loses all its clarity. The exterior spaces loses its void" (*La Poétique* 196).[7] The dialectic between outside/inside for the narrator is no longer based on a reductionist opposition. Rather, it allows us to enter what Bachelard called "the phenomenology of the poetic imagination": "Through poetic language new waves come to the surface of being, and language carries in itself the dialectic of the open and the closed. Through meaning it encloses, through poetic expression it opens" (199). The lyricism in the last pages transmits the feeling of infinity in the narrator's interior space, and the recurring words, such as "incense, perfume, water, affection, fidelity, heat, moisture, sounds of water droplets, pleasure . . ." correspond to the imagination of rest and tranquility. Beatriz wants to enjoy and extend endlessly the limits of the self, to overcome her fear of others and of society, to be equal to her desires and her contradictions. She finds herself afflicted with a touch of "Beylism" (from Henri Beyle or Stendhal) to the extent that she expresses, like the Stendhalian hero, "a certain passion for contradicting oneself, for surprising oneself, for thinking paradoxically, and for antinomies that present themselves and oppose one another with no possible synthesis; madness/reason, passion/irony, pain/pleasure, [Mexico/Italy]" (Crouzet 58). In the final passage described by the narrator, "nothing is heard but the fluttering of butterflies resting on an ear, on my hair. Nothing is seen but the dense perfumed mist of incense. No scent but that of our bodies, our fluids, our desires. What is seen, smelled, and heard are our pleasures" (182). In this "cosmicity of images"

---

[7]In his study of the poetry of Henri Michaux, Bachelard demonstrates how the poet alters the notions of a spatiality defined by a geometry that separates the inside from the outside to the point of mutual exclusion. For Bachelard "the inside and the outside lived by the imagination cannot be considered only according to their mere reciprocity. From that moment, no longer speaking of the geometric to utter the first expressions of being, choosing more concrete, more phenomenologically exact departure points, we realize that the dialectic between inside and outside multiplies and diversifies into innumerable hues" (*La Poétique de l'espace* 196).

is inscribed "the image of being,"[8] the image of *being* Beatriz. In effect, one has to wait until the end of the novel to pronounce the name of the narrator, Beatriz, thus securing her identity before the world.

The name Beatriz explains, in part through its symbolism, the somewhat ambiguous ending of this novel. For any reader familiar with the work of Italian Renaissance poet and writer Dante, Beatriz symbolizes enduring love. Seeing his passion as a source of mystic ascent, the poet makes Beatrice his intercessor in his search for salvation. In the Divine Comedy, she is presented as the emblem of lucidity, the one who guides the soul to the realm of the divine. When Beatrice dies, the poet's love turns to mystic love.[9] The enchanted, almost religious realm that the narrator creates and surrounds herself with ("I have left only my enormous bed, like an altar, in the center of the room") points precisely to the mystical dimension that Beatriz confers on the love she deified: her love for the weekend man.

This love, this "loving too much" of *Demasiado amor*, places the narrator halfway between sublimation and cynicism, and invites us to read the epilogue in various manners. I prefer, however, to interpret it as a rebirth toward a destiny in which Beatriz acts as a participant in and producer of national space. A destiny that draws her closer to, rather than separating her from, the social architecture, the social family represented by her clients of both sexual genders:

---

[8]With respect to the notion of "the image of being," Bachelard writes in his chapter on the "phenomenology of the round" that "being takes a thousand forms, but does not undergo dispersion: if some day one could gather all the images of being in an extensive imagery, all the multiple, changing images which, despite everything, illustrate the permanence of being, the Rilkean tree would open a great chapter in my album of concrete metaphysics" (214). In the case of Beatriz, the butterfly and the fish represent "central images" in the narration. While, according to Bachelard, for Michelet the "model of being" is signified by the bird and for Rilke by the tree, the butterfly and the fish also signify the "model of being" for Beatriz "as it isolates itself, rounds itself" to the point of "taking on the figure of being which centers itself on itself and rounds itself" (214). The narrator explains: "I'm calm like I haven't been in a long time. Perfect calm and absolute silence, with my spirit distant from everything, submersed in an unspeakable serenity" (185).

[9]See in particular Danie Alighieri's *La vita nuova* and the sonnets of the *Canzionere*. In *La divina commedia*, cantos xxx and xxxi of *Purgatorio* are of interest.

"I write this to tell you that at last I have fulfilled my dream of having a boarding house" (183). Faced with the deciphering of her subjective space, the narrator discovers herself as a landscape of multiple strata, jolted by a dynamic tension. This perpetual dynamism allows the narrator-protagonist to weave her destiny, to transcend the notion of irrevocability and fatality. She manages to modify the course of her existence because she lives it, controls it, examines and takes control of it until she rules over it.

The words of the American artist-poet Irene Rice Pereira, collected in her essay *The Nature of Space* (1991) allow us to conclude perfectly, saying that Beatriz, through writing, succeeds in raising herself "to the heights of exaltation in an ever-expanding endeavor to enlarge the small part of space allotted to [her] as [her] share in creation" (50).

Brianda Domecq, with her novel *La santa de Cabora*, also invites us to penetrate and to question the formation of national, historical and geographical space. She creates a narrator-researcherwho endeavors to recount and rewrite the participation of one of the many women protagonists which National History omitted from its pages.

CHAPTER 3: *LA INSÓLITA HISTORIA DE LA SANTA DE CABORA*: FROM THE LOCATION OF MEMORY TO DEMYSTIFICATION

> A story: the important thing is to have a story and keep having a story in order to live. (Wim Wanders, *Wings of Desire*)

By setting her novel *La insólita historia de la Santa de Cabora* (1990) in a particular historical period, Brianda Domecq (b. 1942) travels the same path as several of her contemporaries. Domecq situates her novel in the Porfiriato, the era of President Porfirio Díaz and the Yaqui, Mayo, and Tomochitec Indian resistance movements. This novel stands opposite that of José López Portillo y Rojas, *Parcela* (1898), but echoes that of Heriberto Frías, *Tomóchic* (1893–95), in the way that it questions and refutes the time-honored *pax porfiriana*, unfolding a narrative in which instability prevails. Nevertheless, Domecq's originality surpasses others by virtue of having selected a main character whom John Brushwood and other critics and historians have labelled "a neurotic young woman nicknamed the Saint of Caborca [*sic*]." Teresita or Teresa de Urrea, the Saint of Cabora, is the name that Domecq prefers to bestow upon this historical figure who occupies the central position of her novel.

Before beginning the analysis of the most notable aspects of this novel, it would be appropriate to briefly summarize its plot and the "genesis" of the character Teresa. *La insólita historia* is composed of two texts: one which narrates Teresa's life and the other which relates the inquiries of a researcher who lives in late twentieth-century Mexico City, devoting fifteen years of her life to reconstructing the history of Teresa de Urrea. Teresa, on the one hand, is born in 1873, the illegitimate daughter of Cayetana Chávez, a young Indian woman from Tehueco, and Don Tomás Urrea, a landholder by inheritance, of Spanish blood. She is raised by her mother's family in one of the groves of the Rancho de Santana owned by Don Tomás. In 1880, national elections result in the reelection of Porfirio Díaz. Don Tomás, who had been a fervent supporter of Lerdo, leader of the opposition to Díaz, is persecuted by Díaz after his reelection. In fact, Díaz begins a campaign of reprisals against the Lerdo supporters, which forces Don Tomás, his family, and his laborers to move from Rancho de Santana to Rancho de Cabora in the state of Sonora. Don Tomás's wife, Doña Loreto, and their children prefer luxury and comforts to the rustic pleasures of Cabora, so they choose to live on a third Rancho in los Alamos, some 30 miles from Cabora. Don Tomás, a few years after having settled in Cabora, falls in love with the young Gabriela Cantúa, daughter of a neighboring rancher, and she comes to live with him. Just a few miles away lives Teresa on the impoverished ranch of Aquihuiquichi. At age fifteen, Teresa decides to introduce herself to her father, Don Tomás. He recognizes her as his own and invites her to live with him, Gabriela, and Huila, a healer and housekeeper from Cabora. Shortly after her arrival in Cabora, Teresa displays healing powers which turn Cabora into a site of pilgrimage for thousands of Mexicans, particularly Indians.

Few books were written on the life of Teresa de Urrea. One of the first was *La santa de Cabora* (1902) by Lauro Aguirre, a friend of the Urrea family; unfortunately, this appears to be a "lost" bibliographical item; it is cited by Holden. Teresa was, however, the subject of various articles in the Mexican and U.S. press, in newspapers such as *La opinión*, *El nacional*, *El progresista*, the *San Francisco Examiner* and the *New York Journal*. In 1978, archaeologist and historian William Curry Holden published *Teresita*, a book that narrates in almost novelistic fashion the history of Teresa, her family and the Yaqui, Mayo, and Tomochitec uprisings against the Díaz government. Domecq bases her novel on reports that have been written on Teresa to date. In *La insólita historia*'s title we already see in profile the key question posed by Domecq throughout the narration; namely, to which "history" does this character belong?

The "Locations of Memory"

The semantics of the title itself is rich in signs. The word "insólito" [unexpected, uncommon] refers to the strange, to that which is surprising because of its unusual, uncommon, or rare nature. Until the beginning of the twentieth century, the word "insólito" was filled with bias, and its definition, "contrary to custom," was used in a pejorative sense. As will be seen in my analysis throughout this chapter, Domecq sets out to rehabilitate the word and hence the history of the Saint of Cabora, an uncommon history because it is prodigious, formidable, and positively disconcerting. With the word "history" Domecq introduces the discontinuities between the history of Teresita and the History of the Saint of Cabora, each inseparable from the other. In effect, History represents an indispensable source for discovery, uncovering the Saint's genealogy and hence conjecturing that of Teresita. If the word history is synonymous with story, defined as something invented, improbable, or intended to deceive, to mystify, it should be set opposite

History constituted on the basis of empirical scientific studies of past events. In addition, History is defined as a relation of memorable events, of facts from the past relative to the evolution of humankind worthy or deemed worthy of memory.[1] But what constitutes memorability? What are the events, the persons considered worthy of memory? And who dictates and institutes the criteria for memory? What are the links between memory and history? These are some of the questions that *La insólita historia* tries to answer.

The first pages of the book form a sort of preface, an entry into the subject matter headed by a word taken from the Catholic liturgy: "Introito," a chant meant to be performed before the mass, while the celebrant and his ministers enter. This word refers back to the third word of the novel's title: "Santa." It is not by chance that the preface takes the form of a dialogue between an angel and God, or that it refers to a woman who comes to the doors of paradise and requests permission to enter as the Saint of Cabora. God denies the petition of the Saint of Cabora for two reasons. On the one hand Teresa de Cabora does not have the same status as Teresa de Avila. There is only one Teresa, the one from Avila, from Spain, the cradle of Catholicism. On the other hand, she is a woman. The hope is to establish clearly from the beginning that the life of Teresa was not worthy of a saint, hence the impossibility of listing her in the calendar ("monuments of a historical consciousness" Benjamin, *Illuminations* 261) of the saints. To this is added the misogynistic response of God to the angel, which follows the traditional thinking that the institution of the Catholic church founds its religion one, among other things, ontological categories that separate origin (Adam, paradise) from the cause of loss of origin (Eve):

> Nothing! Tell her she's not listed. Either she's got the wrong year or she's got the wrong heaven. And don't let her cry on you. Women always cry when they don't get what they want; they cry or pray or beg or they get a fake hymen from somewhere to prove they're virgins and therefore martyrs. Nothing. If she resists, ask for her genealogy. Women can never trace their genealogy further than two generations. (6)

Teresa, unruffled, goes on to proclaim her genealogical tree and in this way she disproves God, the creator of the universe. With this allegory, Domecq, from the opening of her novel, makes manifest her wish to denounce the fallacious myths

[1]See De Certeau's "Making History," in *The Writing of History,* trans. and ed. by Tom Conley (1988), 19–55.

which have nourished and continue to nourish our spirits. She begins with the idea that God either lacks the imagination or power—power upon which his divinity is based—to read books, histories, places, or saints not yet written. If the image of God as foundation of truth can be weakened (in an almost Nietzschean fashion) to the point of dissolution, who can stop Domecq and the researcher from venturing onto the rugged trails of "historical truths"?

Cabora: the first part of *La insólita historia* begins with the word "Cabora," the last word of the title, whose functioning is key to the process of demystification that the researcher takes up with relation to what History has recorded of Teresa de Urrea's life. It is not a question here of discovering the truth but rather of uncovering the falsehoods upon which historical truth was based.

Immediately the omniscient narrator allows the reading public to share the intimacy of the researcher's world, guiding the reader in the footprints that will eventually lead to the beginning point of her academic investigation. The complicity set up between the researcher and the reader allows the latter to discover how the idea for this study project originated, and what the object of the research is. We discover that the idea for probing into the life of Teresa de Urrea came in a dream, a dream

> that erupted in her lonely nights like a magical sign, a ciphered sign. It recurred three times in the month of October 1973, the 13th, 14th, and 15th, and was most intense and most distressing the last time, the very day on which the hundredth anniversary of the birthday of Teresita was celebrated. (9)

As Freud stated in *Interpretation of Dreams*,

> . . . one component of the content of the dream is a repetition of a recent impression of the previous day. This impression that is to be represented in the dream may either itself belong to the circle of ideas surrounding the actual instigator of the dream—whether as an essential or as a trivial portion of it—or it may be derived from the field of an indifferent impression which has been brought into connection with the ideas surrounding the dream-instigator by more or less numerous links. (180)

The researcher insists on the premonitory aspect of the dream and her ignorance of Teresa's past life. But the presence of the dream as an event outside the researcher's will and rationality (a dream filled with supernatural phenomena) turns out to be the excuse that she was waiting for to take new directions in her life as a researcher and as a woman. Here the dream is not restricted to being "her sleeping thoughts," rather it refers more appropriately to "her awakening thoughts," to use Paul Valéry's formulation. She herself fills her dreams with the desire of transcending a reality in which she no longer feels she belongs. The appearance of Teresa in her dreams corresponds more to the revelation of a hidden reality, both Teresa's history and that of the investigator, than to the physical manifestation of an invisible being who suddenly becomes visible. In fact, at the end of the novel, throughout which Teresa's specter seems to float, an allusion is made, for example, to a Teresa who is far from being willing to remain in the "paths" of oblivion. The content of the researcher's dream coincides with the materialization of her "political unconscious," which aspires to go beyond History as the "governing and shaping role of national consciousness" (Nora xxi). As Fredric Jameson explains, "the historical *pensée sauvage*, or what we have called the political unconscious, nonetheless seeks by logical permutations and combinations to find a way out of its intolerable enclosure and produce a 'solution'" (167). The dream as home of the *pensée sauvage* constitutes the ideal space for proposing other possibilities, the dream being, as Valéry stated, "a hypothesis, as it is only possible to apprehend it through memory." Hence the dream of the researcher, possibly the product of her political unconscious, becomes what I choose to call the first "location of memory" (a term borrowed from Pierre Nora) of Domecq's novel, within which is found, like a *mise en abyme,* a second location of memory, Cabora:

> At that time I didn't know it, I didn't know anything. The only clue was the dream: she was standing in a desert landscape, an endless plain, dry and arid. In the distance the horizon was visible, its definitive line interrupted only here and there by a rugged stone, a lifeless tree, the soft back of a sand dune rising slightly above the land. . . . She was alone, and faced with the immensity of the severe open space, she felt an enormous fatigue, as though she had walked for days searching . . . for a place called Cabora. (9–10)

As Pierre Nora confirms, "history is the always problematic and incomplete reconstruction of that which is no longer a representation of the past; memory is always a phenomenon of the present, a region experienced in the eternal present" (xix). Constituting Cabora as a region of memory is a way to compensate for its absence in History, in atlases, in encyclopedias, as if its "need of memory were a need of history" (Nora xxv). Thus the memory of the researcher is rooted in the concretion that constitutes the topography of Cabora, a topography delineated first in dreams and then as a visible, palpable space. The description of the researcher's voyage is almost identical to the voyage which Teresa takes in the novel (93, 149). The narrative osmosis which can be perceived between these two characters turns the researcher into a character of fiction and Teresa into a historical figure, while at the same time memory "transforms itself into the object of a possible history" (Nora xxi). The researcher, motivated by her desire to dissolve the opposition between memory and History, travels to Cabora and thus unites toponymy with topography. Therefore, Cabora is presented in the novel as a symbol of narrative temporalities coexisting in a single novelistic time.

The coexistence of different temporalities in a single novelistic time can be explained in the following manner: Julia Kristeva reminds us that time in the novel implies the existence of at least two temporalities. The first is distinguished as the "temporality of narrative enunciation" which is equivalent to the "time of recounted history;" the second corresponds to the "temporality of the word which is spoken, the trajectory of the very utterance" (*Texto de la novela* 249–50). The second temporality refers to the temporality of the distributive utterance, the "mixture of a narrative utterance and a self-referential utterance. It begins with a narration in the past, returning to an utterance in the present, that is, to the word which the subject-author of the literary enunciation gives to the protagonists, subjects of utterance" (*Texto de la novela* 253). What is most interesting about Domecq's novel is that two temporalities of narrative enunciation and consequently two temporalities of utterance are verified, all linked by Cabora as space and geographic scenario. The first corresponds to the time measuring the history of the researcher and the meanderings of her investigation, at the same time giving life to a "distributive utterance" exemplified as follows:

> In the dusty airport of Navojoa only she [the researcher] and two other passengers left the plane. . . . She approached the clerk. . . . When she showed him her counter receipt, he let out a hoot and swatted a fly on the countertop. "It's been more than two months since anyone from that agency has come around here." (66)

The second temporality of narrative enunciation corresponds to the time measuring exclusively Teresa de Urrea's history, which covers the second and third portions of *La insólita historia*. Here is an example of the distributive utterance which is produced:

> She stood in the center of the circle, and stretching as tall as she could,

> she looked at them enraged, one by one. There was a sudden silence. Palomino hung his head in shame. "How much you want to bet that I play the guitar better than any of you and almost as pretty as Anastasio? How much?" (61)

On the subject of this second narrative temporality it might be said that it is presented as a novel within a novel. The approach to and analysis of such narrative temporalities is complicated by an extensive network of intertextualities which, in the first instance, forces the reader to cross the border between the two temporalities of the narrative enunciation. In other words, the reader, in order to enter the novel, must be flexible enough to perform an incessant coming and going between the narrative enunciations and the distributive utterances which the novel's structure requires.

The first part of *La insólita historia* most requires this reading exercise. The two temporalities of narrative enunciation alternate, as well as the two distributive utterances, as well as document fragments, testimonials, newspapers, and essays which in one fashion or another refer to Teresa, and which the researcher has gathered with great perseverance through fifteen years of investigation. These fragments, reviewed on the plane trip to Cabora, introduce the reader to the opinions of the public, political figures, and priests with respect to Teresa and her life. In addition, they reveal how these opinions gradually become truths, which in turn become shapers of the national consciousness; they also reveal the mystifying linkage that occurs as a result. The fruits of her investigation, highlighted in the text with cursive type, inform the reader of the historical and social background in which Teresa lived. Likewise, it allows the reader to develop a critical sense and facilitates the understanding of the second and third parts of Domecq's novel.

The alternation between the narration whose theme is the investigation and that which refers to the fictionalization of Teresa's biography, carries out various functions. Principally, the first narration allows us to understand the researcher's motivations, her method as she investigates and eliminates materials, her emotional state before and during the visit to Cabora, and her goals. But above all it justifies the need for offering the reader a biographical voyage which transcends the disordered, contradictory, mysterious, and fragmentary character of the information which the researcher has gathered. While the data from the archives is essential to the composition of the biography of Teresa, in the same way it could contribute to the biography's failure.

In effect, three events support this idea. First, the end of the first part of *La insólita historia* coincides with the arrival of the researcher in Navojoa (the town one must pass through to arrive at Cabora); second, her arrival in Navojoa also coincides with the loss of her briefcase, which contains her documents, and finally, and most importantly, the loss of the documents coincides with the moment in which she begins to write Teresa's biography, which constitutes the nucleus of the novel's corpus. Slowly, our researcher ceases to exist in order to give way to the manuscript's writer-narrator, a fiction that, in the manner of a palimpsest, erases the first writing, that of the archives, in order to give life to a new text. The loss of the documents forces the researcher to detach herself, to withdraw from that part of herself which is preventing her from launching unprotected and naked into the creative activity of writing. This implies a renunciation of the presence and comforting closeness of "knowledge," a giving up of the tangible in order to confront the unknown. Walter Benjamin, in his essay "The Mimetic Faculty," writes: "'To read what was never written.' Such reading is the most ancient: reading before languages existed, from entrails, stars, or dances. Later, a mediating link came to be used for a new type of reading, from runes and hieroglyphics. It seems fair to suppose that these were steps during which the mimetic gift, which in another time was the foundation of occult practices, entered into the world of writing and of language" (*Reflections* 336). Before reaching the fullness which the act of writing brings, she must pass through a stage of "detoxification" or defamiliarization:

> She arrived finally, soaked in sweat, exasperated by the loss of the briefcase and frightened to find herself in a strange town for reasons that seemed more and more confusing. . . . She felt powerless after the disappearance of the documents. Now nothing made sense. Fragmented recollections of the writings filled her mind again, blurring together hopelessly. (68)

During any stage of detoxification palliatives are required. In the case of the researcher, ingesting the fine, pink dust from the tiny cave overlooking Cabora allows her to finally replace her documents with a more immediate empiricism, that of Cabora: "She observes that the floor of the tiny cave is covered with a fine dust. . . . She takes a little between her fingers and tastes it: it has no flavor. . . . Suddenly, she sees Cabora in every detail, not as she had seen it before, in ruins, nonexistent, but rather as if she were seeing it from the past, through the memories of Teresa" (149). With this act the researcher demonstrates that history "is founded, in the final account, only on that which motivates, a tenuous link, impalpable, barely expressible" (Nora xiii). In addition, the loss of her documents and the text that such a loss engenders (the palimpsest), reminds us that "paper memories" ("memorias de papel") are not indispensable as long as places of memory exist. The palimpsest text—the biography—could also be read as a work which complicates the mere exercise of memory through an interrogatory game which memory plays upon itself (Nora xxxix). The page allowing transition between the novel's first part and the biography allegorizes the corporeal and spiritual osmosis between the researcher and Teresa—the "historicized" figure. These lines that momentarily link Teresa and the researcher will lead us deeper, in the last section of this study, into the formation of the subjectivity of both characters.

Shamanism and Positivism

The second and third parts of *La insólita historia* provide a historical context that goes beyond a mere backdrop. Teresa arrives in Cabora in 1888, during the second phase of the Porfirista dictatorship; the motto "order and progress" gave rise to a government based on exclusion of any Mexican who did not follow the path outlined by this philosophy. With the support of "scientists" (intellectuals, professionals, and capitalist entrepreneurs who advocated a "scientific" governing of the state), the Díaz administration based itself on the positivist theories of Auguste Comte and Herbert Spencer. By their definition, positivism only admits the experimental method and rejects any a priori notion and any universal and absolute concept.[2] The application of certain laws such as the Lerdo Law (law of confiscation of properties) in the name of modern science and materialism led various social groups, particularly the majority agrarian sector in Mexico, to rebel and express their resentment against what Carlos Monsiváis describes as "the bitter transition of an agrarian community from semifeudalism to a difficult modernization" (*La lucha por* 13). As the mineral, merchant, banking, and industrial sectors developed, small agricultural producers found themselves expropriated and replaced by high-production latifundia which functioned for the most part thanks to exploitation of peons who worked under conditions very similar to those of the colonial period. When not entirely forgotten, indigenous workers were used in the construction of railroads or work in mines. This abuse led them

[2]During the second half of the nineteenth century some followers of Comte questioned this definition. The anthology edited by Sybil Acevedo gathers together essays on the division between French positivists which led to their schism into two factions, one religious and the other scientific.

to open rebellion. The workers went from a state of exploitation directly to one of persecution, since their rebellion represented a threat to the political stability and material progress that the Díaz government proposed.[3] In *La insólita historia*, the Yaqui, Mayo and especially Tomochitec (a mestizo people whose heritage is Tarahumara Indian and Spanish) resistance movements and their subsequent repression by the Díaz government covers a period closely linked to the "entrance" of Teresa de Urrea into history and her transformation from a young healer into the Saint of Cabora.

It is precisely during this administration "of order" with scientific and technological aspirations when Teresa discovers her healing powers. In the first part of Domecq's novel we make contact with both figures, Porfirio Díaz and Teresa de Urrea, through the archives found by the researcher. Each of the characters, we notice immediately, is mythologized. Teresa, on the one hand, is described as a possessed saint (45), a fanatic and a spiritualist (47), hysterical and mystical (52), a witch (54), and mad (69). On the other hand, we find (though less frequently) descriptions that present us with a person of innate intelligence (52), whose "only crime was to tell the truth, to proclaim justice, preach goodness, and extend love to her fellow men" (53). In the case of Díaz, commentaries on his magnanimity seem to prevail. He is a "methodical man" of "simple pleasures" (48):

> *Don Porfirio, First Patriot, one of the most righteous and sincere men in all the Latin American countries; with the power of infinite patience, a constant desire to calm our spirits as much as possible, an almost prophetic power to judge actions and anticipate them, a self-mastery and authority unequalled among his fellow citizens. There is no doubt that the nation counts on the Indispensable One who leads us on the road of peace, prosperity and progress.* (29; emphasis in the text)

In the second part of *La insólita historia*, however, a role reversal occurs which coincides with the demythologizing efforts proposed by Domecq. The novel's entirety develops around the opposition which governed the nineteenth (and con-

---

[3]For a history of the Porfiriato see the works of James D. Cockcroft, Leopoldo Zea.

tinues to govern the twentieth) century,[4] between the rational and the irrational, between progress and backwardness, between science and shamanism. The official institutional discourse of the day is juxtaposed against that discourse which narrates the life of Teresa. The official discourse is printed in quotes and/or in cursive, and refers to newspaper clippings of the period. Without a doubt, the press functions here as a source of information establishing the historical and political context; but above all its presence is proof that "journalism was a fundamental pedagogical device in the training of the citizenry . . . which contributes to the production of a field of identity, a national subject" (Ramos 93).

There is no doubt that Teresa, as healer or as Saint, is far from representing the ideal national subject. Her condition as a shaman, since she is endowed with supernatural powers for healing the sick and the power of divining, is generally presented in the press as hostile to rationalism, as a condition that prevents the subject from acting according to logical principles. Her powers are denounced as a result of her intuitionism (the intimate and immediate perception of an idea or a truth, as though it were visible to the naked eye),[5] which was incompatible with the idea of progress and the avant garde. "'This type of sainthood will take us back to the depths of barbarism which our century has struggled to escape' " (343). "This type of sainthood," in effect, has no place in the political and ideological economy of the Porfiriato; nor is it accepted, however, in the Church, even though the latter is the enemy of the government after liberal reforms effected against it.

To counter the calumny and convince the reader of Teresa's powers, Domecq allows herself lengthy and detailed descriptions of her healings. Gradually the flow of words and details open for any doubting reader the possibility of visualizing and conceptualizing these healings, even accepting them as such.

---

[4]During the present decade of the twentieth century, the discovery is being made in the industrialized nations that science and progress were not infallible and did not tend to our well-being alone. This is leading to a reevaluation, though a slow one, of what is defined as "science." Science, like Heidegger's *Wissenschaft*, is moving closer in meaning to "knowledge" and could eventually come to include in its definition any type of knowledge.

[5]See the works of Bergson, who was opposed to scientific and materialist positivism. He saw philosophy as a conscious and deliberate return to the data of intuition. According to him, intuition allows us to coincide with the free and creative movement of life and the spirit. This is based on the philosophy of comprehension, attentive to immediate experience.

At first surprising and mysterious, they become natural; we are in the presence of a Teresa no longer a mystic healer but rather a person who, like anyone else, uses her skill in the service of others. Teresa does not profess miracles; she "**works** from dawn to dinnertime; from five in the afternoon to sunset, day after day" (202; emphasis mine). Teresa is neither completely shaman nor Saint in the Christian sense, but rather the syncretic product of both religious beliefs and of the tensions and mediations between different traditions.

The use of natural elements, such as the red dust from the cave in Cabora, herbs and plants, and the power of her saliva, refer back to shamanistic practices. She learns to be a shaman with the help of Huila. In other words, it is not merely a condition she was born with. Part of her apprenticeship consists, among other things, of curing herself. As Michael Taussig explains in his book on shamanism and colonialism, in many places of Latin America, in order to be a shaman and master the type of supernatural powers that Teresa is endowed with, one must pass through various cycles: that of affliction, that of salvation, and that of transformation (142). The period of affliction occurs for Teresa when she cures Tencha, who is dying in childbirth: "When death entered that woman, you jumped on her like a cat, you grabbed her face and screamed 'Look at me!'. . . Teresa had absorbed the death of the birthing woman and carried it inside herself. Now it was she who would die" (136). The time that passes from the moment in which Teresa absorbs Tencha's death until Teresa's "first death" covers the first step of affliction. Teresa's absence and withdrawal, or her "first death" (which her detractors called a hysteric trance), is the consequence of this first healing, and lasts three months and eighteen days, during which she continues her healing work. The affliction, however, continues to pursue her; she awakes in a state of amnesia, unable to recall what has happened during her "absence." Teresa tries to adapt to the situation, to avoid the fear and wonder into which fate has tossed her, and to adapt to a "new reality created at the margin of her consciousness" (185).

She is not entirely a shaman, as she does not devote herself to a healing based in the worship of nature or in the belief in spirits. Her powers transcend the idea of religiosity as a collection of ritual acts, bound to the conception of a sacred realm different from the profane, and intended to establish contact between the human soul and deities or spirits. What draws her nearest to shamanism are her therapeutic methods, such as the use of herbs and natural products, but above all the fact that she allows evil spirits (such as Tencha's, for example) to enter her, giving away a part of her life in exchange for the pain of others. Like a "sharkskin" her life shrinks to the point of her second death. Her deeds as a healer recall the emphasis that the Christian religion places on the virtue of charity, and are very similar to the obligation or need the healer has to care for the poor. As Michael Taussig reminds us, the power of any religion is inseparable from its "dialectical relationship with illness and disgrace" (Taussig 158-59). This explains the fact that the Yaqui Indians christen Teresa "the Saint of Cabora," a product of the religious and cultural syncretism from which they themselves also emerge. She is a Saint because she inspires veneration through her exemplary goodness and through her unique virtue for the healing of illnesses. Moreover, the Yaqui need to create a cult, to honor someone as their "mother," the foundation of the Yaqui nation. The unique nature of the resistance movement makes the creation and construction of a spiritual leader, distinct from that of other Mexicans, necessary here. The Virgin of Guadalupe was unable to fill that role, since in one way or another she symbolizes a Mexican nation in which the Yaqui do not feel included. By refusing to accept the national future proposed for them, the Yaqui are in need of a virgin whose therapeutic virtues are foreign to those proposed by the policy of order and progress. Religious syncretism or not, in the same way as shamans were considered the principal obstacles during the conquest (see Taussig 376), the "saint" in times of positivist reform is synonymous with historical aberration. It is precisely this idea of historical aberration that Domecq hopes to defamiliarize in the reader.

Domecq juxtaposes the historical biography of Díaz and that of Teresa to demonstrate that the politics which Díaz practiced were based on methods and beliefs which he himself denounced. While Teresa works to save lives from the feudalism of irrationality, Díaz (Herod, to the indigenous rebels) is represented as a manipulative assassin who protects himself by raising the banner of order, reason, peace and law. While the press presents Teresa as illiterate, the narration highlights the illiteracy of Díaz (65). More interesting, however, is the semantic inversion that operates within the text. The signifiers "miracle" and "prophecy" which appear in the newspaper or archive quotes collected by the researcher suddenly acquire a positive value. Moreover, they seem to be inseparable from the idea of progress. In the same fashion, the aura of mystery and secrecy (31), denounced so fervently as damaging in the case of Teresa, acquires a sense of necessary urgency, to keep the civilizing process alive and healthy, when referring to Díaz. While Díaz, when addressing the citizens, uses a vocabulary nearer to theology or metaphysics than to science, Teresa, addressing the sick, uses a precise, concrete, almost technical language:

> The priest would say: ‘By the will of God it’s not raining, and it will rain again when he wills it: we must pray’. All of this, Teresa explained, was a lie. The rain and drought didn’t depend on God, but on

> the climate. . . . She expressed herself only in the least spiritual and magical form that she knew. She spoke of the phenomenon of rain and of its excesses and absences. She spoke of wind and ocean currents, warm and cold fronts, relative humidity, spontaneous condensation, gradual evaporation, until she knew no more. (207–208)

Such role inversions, in which Díaz becomes what he denounces (that is, a prophet who seeks to do miracles saving Mexicans from the prevailing barbarism), have the function of erasing and eradicating the boundaries between discourses considered incompatible. Domecq denounces the separation of two sciences which language alone separates, a language which, according to Huila, falsifies everything by insisting on a fixed semanticization at any cost: "The problem, child, is words: language doesn't bring us closer to reality, it hides reality" (133). Domecq seeks the fusion of the "forces of Modernity," in this case Díaz and his government, with the forces that deny fixed semanticization, an empiricism that gels only in language or in an invented rationalism. She buries once and for all the idea that rationalism is a invention vital for those who prefer to keep their distance from the excesses at the boundaries separating the spiritual, the sensual, the inexplicable though physically palpable, from the limitations of human understanding and their epistemological system.

The power of Teresa rests not on the word, but resorts to another sense, that of sight/vision, a theme the importance of which I will investigate later. Hence, the functions of expressing thought and communicating transcend vocal or graphic signs. For Teresa, language is not the only means to materialize thought and power. Nevertheless, though the expression of her medical terminology is very different from that which the Porfiriato would impose, she also seeks improvement of the human condition. Domecq demonstrates that the means employed by Díaz to reach Modernity lead to the marginalization of the widest sector of the Mexican populace, in other words, those who, since the conquest, have been "processed as primitives through a variety of tropes in which they are seen as a threatening herd, a faceless, promiscuous mass, reproducing, inferior and even exterminable" (Torgovnick 18). Many passages describe and document repression. But Domecq's text goes beyond a mere demonizing of Díaz's government. It seeks to recall also that the contours of the Porfirian economy look too much like those of the colonial past, whose ideology—that civilization and progress are privileges of the West—only allowed entry into the civilized family to those who unconditionally obeyed its rules and norms. In Díaz's system, those who withdraw from the genetic and cultural norms constituting Modernity risk scientific and technological backwardness and are condemned to remain in a state of underdevelopment. Hence the notion of the "indigenous" gives rise to the idea of lack of modern technology: Domecq endeavors to demonstrate that responsibility for the destruction of indigenous peoples falls on the blind desire for Modernity and not on Teresa's powers.

Domecq's novel asks the question "what is meant by modern technology?" As Martin Heidegger stated, the word "technology" comes from the ancient Greek word *techné* which, in the same way as science and metaphysics, is a "way of revealing" (xxviii). As various critics have pointed out, Heidegger did not limit the concept of technology to the idea of mechanization or automation, rather, by technology he meant a constant challenge, "a challenge that presents itself as such when energy, hidden in nature, reveals itself, when this discovered energy is transformed to then be collected or stored, distributed or changed" (16). If we agree with Heidegger that revelation is inseparable from nature as "a storehouse, a permanent reserve of energy" (21), and that the challenge resides in "discovering, transforming, storing, distributing and changing," then Teresa and what she represents belongs undeniably to or responds to the technological economy. Whether it be her powers (healing faculties) or her herbs, whose medicinal properties are also used, these are equivalent to energies, at first hidden, which are revealed. From the moment in which these energies are revealed until the moment of healing, Teresa passes through stages identical to those referred to by Heidegger.

The Porfiriato refuses to extend the limits of an epistemological system whose effective force depends on the preservation of the idea of its own superiority. The indigenous resistance, and by extension Teresa's, no longer responds to a primary reaction to the phenomenon of civilization and progress, the justification on which the Díaz government based itself to tighten the repression. The resistance springs instead from the danger carried within the advent of technology. This advent, Heidegger argued, "threatens the act of revealing. It threatens revelation with the possibility that any act of revealing may be consumed by the process of **ordering**, and that things may only reach existence through the clarity manifested by permanent reserve" (33; emphasis mine).[6] The populace rebels against the union between order and progress: "The 'ordering' attitude of modern

---

[6]Heidegger clarifies what he means by the concept of "permanent reserve" (*bestand*) as follows: "In all places, everything is ordered in order to be present, available; to stand alone per se requires additional ordering. . . . It designates nothing less than the way in which it witnesses everything that is caused by the challenging revealing" (17).

science and the way it has of *representing* pursues and encloses nature as a collection of forces of measurable coherence" (Heidegger 21). From a practical point of view, the indigenous peoples read the word "order" not as an intelligible relationship among a plurality of terms, nor as a distribution, a sense of public safety, or social stability; rather they read it as a commandment, an imposition that requires unconditional obedience. The indigenous peoples resist "through the irrationality that is self-defense, against the capitalist rationale presented as the advancement of civilization" (Monsiváis, *La lucha* 13).

An irony prevails in *La insólita historia*, which endeavors to disjoin several common sites. First, the nexus between signifier (civilization) and signified (advancement, evolution, progress) is not always proven, since the word has been a banner for recording colonization and justifying countless holocausts. As long as the miracle of science is believed and defended within the borders of the state sphere, the miracles of a science which disturbs and fails to mesh with the ideas of national development will be condemned: "She let herself be convinced because it was all clear then: these were the days in which she healed while Díaz's men murdered" (339). Second, Domecq questions the systematic attribution of masculine gender to scientific discourse. Here Díaz and Teresa share the same space, that of the novel, though History prohibited Teresa from figuring in the same domain as Díaz. From my previous arguments, it will be clear that Teresa is as legitimate as Díaz, since her miracles "revive" while those of Díaz give rise to "atrocities provoked by pseudoscientific, merely economic criteria (Pani in Montalvo 41). Moreover, Domecq continues the role reversal to the point of demonstrating that Teresa's being labelled as hysterical or possessed, a label historically assigned to women, is more appropriate in this case for the majority of the male figures in the novel.

Díaz and his government suffer from an acute neurosis produced by the anxiety of losing power and of experiencing failure. The narration paints the portrait of an underachieving Díaz, unable to redefine his motto of order and progress when serious social problems appear. Rather than rethink his program for economic development, he sinks into an inflexible rigidity that leads to the mechanical and systematic implementation of a program whose contours leave much to be desired. Such stubbornness and his obvious limitations lead him to compensate for his vulnerability with acts of repression against any citizen who opposes his plans. In the case of Teresa, he first undertakes a campaign of defamation. The inefficacy of the campaign points to the diminishing of his supremacy, a situation that he cannot accept. He exiles Teresa to a foreign country, stripping her and her family of their most elemental rights as Mexican citizens.

Another example of male hysteria is that of Teresa's first husband,

Guadalupe Rodríguez, who on the day of his wedding to Teresa is transformed into an alienated and violent beast. Despite his love for her, Lupe the "macho" feels obligated to challenge her: "We're going to Mexico now, you understand?" (357). Teresa manages to escape from her husband. When he appears at the Mexican border he is jailed for dementia, which leads him to take his own life. Don Tomás, Teresa's father, also reacts pathologically by turning to drink. He remains mute for days and nights, locked in his library when he feels powerless against Teresa. In this novel, instability and vulnerability are, more appropriately, the lot of males, while Teresa is characterized by her resistance, both physical and moral, by her capacity for adaptation, by the unlimited nature of her future. Returning to Taussig's formula, one might say that Teresa and the narration around her can be read as "an allegory against the inherent order in the process of civilization" (390).

Nevertheless, that which is most prominent and most often denounced in this narration is the manipulation which Teresa is subjected to not only by her enemies but also by her allies.

Mythification, Commodification, and Fetishization

The three notions making up the above subheading are ineluctably bound together in this novel. Before beginning the analysis proper of the articulation of these modalities, it would be appropriate to explain or define what is meant by myth, commodity, and fetish.

Myth by definition is characterizedby a construction of the spirit. Myth refers to a representation of real deeds or figures deformed or magnified by the collective imagination and by tradition. I agree, however, with Barthes who adds another dimension to the definition, presenting myth as a "type of speech chosen by history [which] cannot possibly evolve from the 'nature' of things" (*Mythologies* 194). In other words, myth cannot be thought of outside of a semiological system:

> Mythical speech is made of a material which has already been worked on so as to make it suitable for communication: it is because all the materials of myth (whether pictorial or written) presuppose a signifying consciousness, that one can reason about them while discounting their substance. . . . But myth is a peculiar system, in that it is constructed from a semiological chain which existed before it. . . . (195, 199)

As for the word commodity, one would have to say that it includes the idea of advantage, opportunity, facility, and above all utility, availability, and function. Finally, in order to establish the nexus between the word fetish and the definitions used for commodity and myth, I refer to its etymology. Jean Baudrillard, in *For a Critique of the Political Economy of the Sign*, reminds us that the word fetish originally meant fabrication, a labor of appearancesand signs. He adds that the word appears in France in the seventeenth century and acquires the sense it had in Portuguese (*feitiéo*, from latin *factitius*), "imitation by signs." Baudrillard attributes the origin of the Spanish word *afeitar* to *feitiéo*, which explains the emergence of the sense of "to paint, adorn, embellish" and for *afeite* the sense of "preparation, ornamentation, cosmetics" (91). The idea of artificiality, falsification, imitation and imposture is of interest here. In the same way in which myth is the product of a collection, a combination of elements indispensably associated, fetishism is also grounded within a system which Baudrillard prefers to call a code: "It is not the passion (either of objects or subjects) for substances that speaks in fetishism, it is the *passion for the code*, which, by governing both objects and subjects, and by subordinating them to itself, delivers them up to abstract manipulation" (92). What then joins these three concepts in *La insólita historia* and even establishes their interdependence is the idea of fabrication, deformation, artificiality, and association. Hence a commodity lends itself to fetishism and the fetishization of a commodity easily becomes myth.

The narration shows how Teresa falls prey to this type of interweaving or meshing. In fact, it generates one of the most important themes of this novel. Teresa moves through the text as an object of convenience or a commodity for the government, for Lauro Aguirre, and for the indigenous peoples, and finally for the United States. It might seem contradictory that Teresa should be a commodity for Díaz and his government, since they seek to eliminate her. Nevertheless, Teresa embodies the ideal signifier for the creation of a myth. If, as Barthes affirms, the function of myth is at first to distort and not to make disappear, it is understood that the Porfiriato has not chosen to ignore her. She represents, in reality, the sign necessary for the emergence of the myth of order and progress.[7] Here the press serves the government as a location for mythic speech. The incorporation of period press extracts in the novel allows us to become mythologists,

[7]Barthes holds that certain myths, like anything else, require space to mature. The myth of order is one myth which, according to Barthes, develops and is perfected in an especially apt fashion among the bourgeoisie and petit bourgeoisie (237).

that is to say, studious readers of myths and not just "readers" of myths. For the reader of myths, Barthes explains, it is as if "the picture *naturally* conjured up the concept, as if the signifier *gave a foundation* to the signified" (216). The reader of myths is a consumer, while the mythologist demystifies. But what is the signified or concept necessary for "uttering" the myth of order and progress? And how is such a myth shaped in the written text of the press? The concept obviously refers back to the power of the government and its policy. A brief approach to the language-object ("the language which myth gets hold of in order to build its own system" (Barthes 200) will allow me to reveal how one arrives at metalanguage, at myth. As a result of the above, one can conclude that the language used in the government press to describe Teresa and her activities is defamatory. Teresa is an impostor, a charmer, a witch, a madwoman, irrational, illiterate (31), a threat to the public peace (54). This image is set against that of Díaz. The language describing the latter leaves no doubt (29). It is composed of an affirmative discourse (28) directly quoting the words of Díaz (49) while at the same time resorting to a legalistic, imperative style (53) that justifies everything through the universality in which it attempts to dress itself (221). The type of association produced in the myth reader's mind, as "confused and shapeless" as it might be, and whose "unity and coherence are above all due to its function" (Barthes 204), posits a "knowledge, a past, a memory, a comparative order of facts, ideas, decisions" (Barthes 202). Díaz and his government exploit the binarisms of rationality/irrationality, legality/illegality, truth/lie, progress/backwardness (and not progress versus tradition, being much less manipulable), all binarisms which at the end of the nineteenth century in Mexico were only beginning to be questioned. The myth of order and progress and of its universality uses Teresa as an "instrumental signifier" in order to establish itself.

Lauro Aguirre, an engineer, erudite, a friend of the Urrea family, and above all a leader of one the centers of resistance against the Díaz government, also uses the press to broadcast his opinions.[8] He also exploits, however, his friendship with the Urrea family for his "paper revolution":

---

[8]The novel points to the widespread use of the press by both the government apparatus and its opponents. Moreover, the novel crosses borders and shows that the manipulation favored by the press is not exclusive to Mexico. In fact, even in a democracy like the United States, the press turns out to be very similar to Mexico's. The press as an apparatus of mythification *par excellence* "highlights the importance of writing for the regulation and definition of the national space" (Anderson in Ramos 93). The sensationalist dimension of the North American press is obvious (319).

> His blood boiled with desires of seeing fulfilled the predictions he daily made for himself or for others of an armed uprising that would overthrow the dictator, murderer of women and children. But despite the signs that followed one after another, something was lacking: a unifying element for all the outbreaks that would give direction to the movement. Lauro decided to create one. (244–45)

In his pamphlets Aguirre describes Teresa "preparing herself for her role in the coming revolution. Her spirit is growing stronger, and the day will come when she will rise up to ignite the souls of the repressed and the weak and turn them into heroes" (245–46). Ignoring all Aguirre's journalistic conspiracies, Teresa is transformed into a spiritual leader in spite of it all. Aguirre does not restrict himself to the press apparatus: he commodifies Teresa through another signifier, that of photography. Under the pretext of getting Teresa and her family out of their financial difficulties at the beginning of their stay in the United States, Aguirre decides to dress her as a saint, take her photograph and sell it as a religious relic:

> From the beginning, he had considered the exile of the Urrea family as a stroke of luck for his cause, but he knew he had to involve them little by little, without pressure. . . . Teresa would be the living symbol that would channel the movement; the innocent victim; the pure virgin; the banner that would raise the whole nation behind him, as it had risen behind the Virgin of Guadalupe. (297)

There is no doubt that Aguirre sees myth "as the experience of history within the configuration of a changing present necessary to development and its revolution" (Taussig 167). Teresa and her myth represent for Aguirre the only force against hegemony capable of galvanizing the indigenous peoples and creating problems for the Díaz government. To create a consumable myth, however, the fraud must be a convincing one. Aguirre chooses photography because in and of itself "there's no more convincing fraud" (Desnoes 384). In part, it is convincing because, as Georges Didi-Huberman explains, "photography is, in spite of everything, always vouched by truth. Not the truth of the senses but the truth of existence, since it is assumed that photography always authenticates the existence of its referent" (63). Aguirre's photograph is doubly fraudulent because the existence of the referent, the evidence (Teresa dressed as a saint) is a simulacrum even before it is captured by photographic vision: the image of Teresa is a simulated simulacrum.

In his essay "The Work of Art in the Age of Mechanical Reproduction," Benjamin points out that "photographic reproduction . . . can capture images which escape natural vision . . . can put the copy of the original into situations which would be out of reach for the original itself" (*Illuminations* 220). He also points out that photography replaces a unique existence, its history, its peculiarities, its fullness, with a plurality of copies of that existence (*Illuminations* 221). Nevertheless, it is worth mentioning that here photography corresponds neither to a copy of an original nor to a reproduction of something authentic. Photography as a technology is not what alters Teresa's authenticity; rather it is the photograph as a form or signifier of the myth that Aguirre wants to create that has the function of commodification. It permits, on the one hand, the fetishism of the commodity, and on the other, the immobilization of Teresa's falsified image, the double simulacrum necessary to the constitution of the myth. Baudrillard is correct in writing that "fetishization of the commodity is the fetishization of a product emptied of its concrete substance. . . . It is an active, collective process of production and reproduction of a code, a system" (93). The photograph freezes Teresa as the object of a lasting image, available for consumption by anyone, for appropriation through fetishization. In the same way, Teresa's image can not function without simplifying her, impoverishing her personally. In fact, for Aguirre, the reader of the myth would have to read the signified, the concept of the myth, as follows: "the revolution is alive and is our only hope, our last resort." He devotes himself to sanctifying the revolution, but to do so he must first sanctify Teresa. Aguirre chooses photography as a language because pictures as language are more imperative than writing (Barthes 195). In the end, myth "interpellates," "designates," "notifies," and above all "imposes." For this reason the iconographic composition, whose result takes shape in the materiality of the photograph, is so carefully constructed: "To play your role in society you have to dress like the character" (298).

Nothing is lacking in this photograph, and Teresa's transformation, without a doubt, moves in what Barthes calls a mythological routine.[9] First, Teresa's body is posed. Her body and in particular her face are presented to the

[9]The mythological routine in which Teresa's transformation moves is very similar to that of l'Abbé Pierre, which Barthes analyzes in *Mythologies*. Barthes' work as a mythologist in "Iconographie de l'Abbé Pierre" has been very useful in the present study.

view obliquely, as if the subject of the portrait consisted of a "quasi-visage."[10] Aguirre dresses Teresa in a long, tight black dress, that makes her look very thin. This confers a seriousness and sobriety on her, the asceticism proper to sainthood, while her thinness points to her frugality and her apostolic poverty. Her hair pulled back tightly and knotted at the nape of the neck, her forehead bared to be seen better (299) all give her an air of neutrality and severity and move her closer to the "chapel archetype" of sainthood. Her gaze, the power of which is decisive in Teresa's life, is also falsified through the makeup worn so that her eyes seem larger and sadder. This gaze signifies humility and heavenly piety, a gaze untouched by earthly corruption. Finally, the crucifix and rosary added to the composition are the most recognizable signs of Christian and especially Catholic faith. The crucifix in particular refers back to Calvary and the condemned Christ's martyrdom, and it reminds us by extension of the persecution and exile which Teresa has suffered.

This composition awakens or revives Catholicism in the Mexican inhabitants of the northern border region, a Catholicism which in the United States is widely overshadowed by Protestantism. At the same time, it establishes a link between the idea of independence and that of religion, between the building of the Mexican nation and devotion and religiosity, a link which the scientific government of Díaz tried to eradicate at all cost. With this strategy, Aguirre hopes to bring more people into the cause. Teresa's image inspires compassion in a populace that identifies with the feeling of solitude and anonymity which living in a foreign land and culture implies. Aguirre is counting on the feeling of solidarity from people who know how long and difficult the voyage to exile can be. He hopes to touch and stir emotions, to the point of producing nostalgia for the native land and its culture in which "they wanted an identity as a people, they wanted new myths, they wanted to reinvent lost traditions in order to feel that they belonged somewhere, to some history" (294).

---

[10]"Quasi-visage" is a French term which Didi-Huberman borrows from Sartre's *Imaginaire* (1940). See page 84. Didi-Huberman's work provides a penetrating critique of the use of photography in Charcot's therapeutic and pedagogic project in his study of hysteria. Didi-Huberman describes the poses of Charcot's patients as a "drama, that is to say the struggle of the subject with the picture taken of him, subjecting the subject to the semblance of a quasi-visage, as through a quasi-homicide" (*L'Imaginaire* 108). I reiterate here the idea that we are in the presence of a double drama, since the subject, Teresa, struggles with a dual composition of images: first with the saintly image created by Lauro before the pose and then with the image of the pose captured in the photograph.

The Yaqui Indians, before Teresa is exiled, also dress her as a deity, entertain her for three days, and crown her Queen of the Yaquis. The press takes advantage of this moment to take their first photograph of her:

> By the third day, Teresa was so tired that she didn't even notice when they took her photograph. A week later Lauro arrived with the newspaper: on the front page, eight columns wide, it read "Teresa Urrea named Queen of the Yaquis" and below was the photo of her dressed as a bride, with a wreath of flowers on her head, her arms extended to give the celebrants a blessing. (220)

Here a double commodification of Teresa very similar to that perpetrated by Aguirre is verified. In this case the first commodification occurs with the costume placed on Teresa by the Yaquis; the second occurs when the press immobilizes the image which all factions can then mythify to their liking. The photo functions as an instrument which allows not only Teresa's manipulation, but also that of the populace, who equate the photo with a "must-read of identity in the image."[11] Domecq elaborates on the problem of excessive adulation of the signifier over the signified.

Teresa's commodification in the United States gives rise to other myths. The medical company that hires her in San Francisco sponsors public gatherings of 1,500 persons, in which Teresa displays her healing power. The company charges the patients she sees "in violation of contract" (376). They hope, moreover, to produce in the patient and/or myth reader the association necessary for the creation of the next myth: "Teresa uses our products to heal. Buy our products and we guarantee your cure." Likewise, Teresa's function, again an "instrumental signifier," is to appease and give hope to those who have not yet passed from traditional to more modern medicine. She serves as a mediator between two epistemological systems whose coexistence is problematic. Here Teresa, the object of an "image-maker," is instrumental in the marketing of medications; through her the art of appealing psychologically to the public with commercial aims is practiced. Teresa enters the world of advertising and she enters a period when the art of "manufacturing" men and women is being perfected. Whether in photographs or in the staging-exhibition of her talents, Teresa's presence and her

---

[11]See the disturbing analysis by Didi-Huberman of the use of photography as a means of identification, and what he calls the "subtle complicity" established between the medical and law enforcement professions.

image are suggestive and captivating. Nevertheless, the importance of the coming of technology to Teresa's life can not be ignored.

In Mexico, Teresa represents a tradition which the Díaz government views as an obstacle to proposed economic development. The United States, on the other hand, with its strong imperialist history,[12] appropriates Teresa's "authenticity" and capitalizes her in hopes of achieving an industrialization and mechanization still perceived as alienating (in the sense of *Entfremdung*, from Marx and Hegel) a semblance of humanity and belonging. The medical firm exploits Teresa's financial need and counts on popular belief in myths. Moreover, it is important to remember that a good number of these beliefs in the Western world are ineluctably linked to the ambiguous image which colonization has constructed of the indigenous person in the mind of the "civilized" person. It is not surprising, therefore, that the public willingly consumes Teresa's actions, words and healings, "objectifying their fantasies" in her discourse (Taussig 8).

In *La insólita historia*, Domecq is generous with details when revealing the exploitation and manipulation of which Teresa is object. Nor does she confine herself to a purely historical reevaluation. To complete the process of demystification, Domecq seeks to join Teresa's public life to her private life. Gradually, she leads the reader through the novel to discover another world: Teresa's subjectivity and its unfolding.

Who is Teresa? Subjectivity and Osmosis

I showed earlier Aguirre's use of photography as a device commonly associated with the idea of "real." Likewise I mentioned that the process of composition preceding the photograph is invisible, hidden to the viewer looking at the photo. For this reason, what the viewer sees is the artifact, the photograph, which only "captures the moment, thus cutting off the past and the future" (Silverman, "What is a Camera" 32). Domecq attempts to demonstrate that history failed or refused

[12]This also explains, however, the rejection of some Mexicans living in the U.S. toward their recently arrived compatriots, which comes about as a result of a feeling of inferiority and a desire for integration with the new culture in which they live. In the novel, several allusions are made to the fear of some "Mexican families being identified as Indians. They aspired, more than anything, to erase their mestizo features, to learn English, to conceal their Latino origin and to be accepted by the whites, or at least by the Hispanics, who claimed to be direct descendants of the Spanish" (295).

to differentiate between Teresa and Teresa's picture, between the photograph-identity and Teresa's identity, a history that refused to see what "lay hidden" behind the image of the image. Domecq demonstrates that photography is "an antirealist representational system" which history used to Teresa's detriment, a system capable not only of "kidnapping the real by putting an image in its place" (Silverman 1993, 33), but also of kidnapping in a similar fashion the simulacrum and superimposing upon it its own image. As a response to this failure, Teresa's healing powers acquire a materiality in *La insólita historia*, an efficacy that surpasses the empiricism of photography. That which is supposedly esoteric and indecipherable becomes more legible, more *visible*, while that which is empirical and technological pretends, hides, and distorts to the point of mortifying. In fact, as Silverman postulates, "the memorial function of photography is imbricated so faithfully with its mortifying effect that it is finally transformed into an ideal agent for the representation of all that which has fallen under a death sentence" (33).[13]

One can verify immediately that Teresa has been sentenced to death many times in many ways: by Díaz, who slandered and discredited her before exiling her from Cabora and her life; by the Indians and Cruz Chávez, chief of the Tomochitecs, who sanctify her against her wishes and hold her captive through an alienating image; by Aguirre, who carries out the first two death sentences by fixing them in the photograph and his press articles. One could almost see Teresa as a character confined to occupy the space of death. But then, who is Teresa of Cabora? That Domecq would give no definitive answer to this question was to be expected. She chooses to create a character whose subjectivity takes shape in a constant doing and undoing, a subjectivity barely established at the end of her short life. Moreover, Domecq does not restrict herself to Teresa's public self, rather the novel creates a space which allows the cohabitation of the public and private selves.

The nexuses between the different phases of articulation of Teresa's intimate self materialize in the text through the anaphora "the day of her second death." The anaphorical and metaphorical expression marks the beginning of many of the chapters, and is always followed by a conditional verb: "The day of

---

[13]Silverman's reading of the Farocki film *Bilder der Welt und Inschrift des Krieges* has been especially useful here in articulating the idea of photography as a product of mechanical reproduction which does not limit itself to immortalization, but rather implies in and of itself the notion of "devitalization." See Metz, cited in the same article.

her second death she would remember the time of her enclosure" (280). Domecq hopes to transcend the writing of Teresa's past, a past created by the present, and she answers the desire to write the past of Teresa's future, in other words, the past of a time yet to be created. The day of her first death does not become an anaphorical expression, as it coincides with Teresa's arrival in Cabora and her first healing. The first death represents the passage from an autonomous and rebellious life[14] to a life in which her subjectivity finds itself gradually under siege by wishes, desires, and goals imposed upon her. The day of her second death, on the other hand, begins another life. For Teresa, doors are opened onto an awakening of subjective experience, which since the day of her first death had been buried, mortified. On the day of her second death, the past of her future could be written in many ways and could give rise to many interpretations and subjectivities. Domecq chooses to narrate, to imagine one of the possible subjectivities of Teresa, turning on the light and allegorizing her gaze. She comes out to meet a gaze which photography and History forced her to turn away.

During the first stage of her life Teresa learns, from the gaze emanating from her eyes, that each of us depends "on the other not only for our meaning and our desires, but also for the confirmation of our selves" (See Lacan in Silverman, 1993 12). She realizes that the power of the gaze is within her reach. It is not merely fortuitous that Teresa first experiences this power over male characters surrounding her, as a manifestation of her enmity with the reigning system of power. Her first experience is with her cousin who repeatedly needles her, reminding her that "she doesn't even know how to read or write" (147). The next experience is with Palomino who believes her incapable of playing the guitar. Her final experience is with Gabriela's cousin. On this occasion Teresa and her friends invite the cousin and his friends to sing together. The cousin refuses to sing with the girls, claiming that "that stuff is sissy stuff" (147) and that he prefers to armwrestle. In all three cases Teresa, with her gaze, immobilizes and forces those who will not take her seriously (being a woman) to lower their heads and surrender. When she sees, for example, that the cousin's game is attracting more attention than hers, she challenges the cousin: "The cousin prepared for battle. He took Teresa's hand. He had barely done so when he found himself with the back of his own hand on the table. . . . We're done with this

---

[14]With this observation we don't intend to diminish or reduce the sensation of boredom or "sameness" and dissatisfaction that invades Teresa as she grows up on the rancho in Aquihuiquichi. This period is a crucial time of apprenticeship, of self-knowledge in which Teresa is free to decide her own future.

foolishness, we're going to sing a while" (147–48). We are no longer in the presence of a female gaze used as an instrument of resistance. Rather, this is a gaze that assaults and is aware of its determining power over the other. In these instances, the gaze serves not only to weaken but also to demystify the idea of power as an exclusively male phenomenon. To prove this equality, however, Teresa feels obligated at first to repeat steps traditionally considered as masculine:

> She threatened him with a look the way she imagined Don Tomás would do with any subordinate. (58)
> She wanted to be Don Tomás, to have his power and his authority; to earn the respect he earned and cause the fear he caused. . . . The image she had of herself was his image, but without the moustache. (75)

Her attitude at first holds her captive in a system in which the male gaze continues to constitute her self. In effect, no matter how much she succeeds in bending the male will with her gaze, it is that same will that creates, defines, and conditions her gaze, thus maintaining intact the binarization of sexual gender roles and the regulating and coercive sense of the concept of power. Two older women, first Rosaura and then Huila, help Teresa to mature and overcome the "masculinist signifying economy" (Butler's terms, *Bodies That Matter* 13). Rosaura teaches her that it is not enough to absorb every detail of male life in order to be or become someone. She teaches her to read and write with the help of newspaper articles. Reading allows Teresa to develop her historical and political education (the journalistic intertextuality likewise allows the reader access to more information on the period). Huila, for her part, makes Teresa aware that one does not toy with the power of the gaze, but rather utilizes it at opportune moments for the purpose of edifying and constructing, not damaging or eliminating.

Claude Gandelman, in his study *Le Regard dans le texte*, recalls that in Egypt the hieroglyph representing "the self-generated divine god," "the creator," "maker of heaven and earth," takes the form of an eye. He adds that the verb "to make" nearly always includes the sign of the eye, the eye as "symbol of the performative" (11). Moreover, Gandelman, in the introduction to his work, refers to the difference proposed in art history between the optical eye and the tactile eye. The optical eye corresponds to the eye which "skims in a linear and superficial fashion" (17). The tactile eye "penetrates deeply, haptically, it hangs on volumes, on textures" (17).[15] In order to explain the concept of the tactile eye, Claude Gandelman resorts again to hieratic writing, observing that the eye often comes provided with a hand or an arm, the symbol of life: "The eye carries life. The eye touches things. The eye creates by mere contact. . . . The Egyptian eye commands the hand, the hand as appendage, totally and absolutely" (12–15). With the help of Huila, Teresa's eye grows more tactile day by day, more life-creating as it penetrates and absorbs the death and disease it touches. The tactile vision of Teresa's eye not only touches with the hand, but also with the tongue and its motions. Teresa's eyes, and by extension her gaze, do not abuse; rather, they become providers. The apprenticeship teaches Teresa that the power of the gaze is one to be channeled with diligence and caution. Likewise, she uses her ocular energy to direct herself toward her internal light. She questions herself, challenges her own abilities, evaluates her actions and healings and her impact on those who believe in her. But the gratification brought by the effects of her tactile vision do not satisfy her: "She lacked nothing: everything she had desired in life she had reached. But deep inside she felt alone. . . . She could no longer see the future clearly; had she lost the way? Was it simply that she had reached the end, and from now on, days would go on repeating one another monotonously?" (253).

Teresa is diametrically opposed to Díaz, who defines himself by his authority, his supremacy, and the imposition of his dominion over others. Teresa, on the other hand, struggles so that her strength and superiority do not take control of her life and her self. She asks herself "what would her supposed powers be used for if she didn't even know who she was, what she was doing, and what consequence it would have?" (241).

She battles to keep from being totally enveloped by rhetoric, history, and narrative, all patriarchal. The constitutive process of Teresa's subjectivity is a shifting one. It does not reject elements external to her subjectivity which nevertheless constitute it. What she refuses to accept is being enclosed in a spiritual, mystical world: "Three times she publicly denied being a saint and she asked not to be called one, that she was as human as anyone else" (227). Domecq emphasizes this notion of humanity. Analyzing the narration of the encounter between Teresa and Cruz Chávez, it would not be hyperbole to state that the joy Teresa experiences cannot be defined merely as mystical joy, as the latter corresponds to that which is "experienced without the subject being aware of its origin or its

---

[15]The word haptic comes from the Greek *haptesthai*, to touch, or *haptikos*, able to grasp.

nature" (Smith 102). This is instead a simulacrum of mystical joy, a simulacrum necessary to the preservation of Teresa's aura of sainthood. What Teresa experiences is highly sensual and tactile. In Chávez's presence Teresa "fell under the influence of an enormous arousal. . . . She had the inexplicable desire to touch that man, not the way she touched her patients, but as a friend, a brother, a . . ." (224). The ellipsis at the end points to the hesitation Teresa experiences when facing unfamiliar emotions that she immediately associates with the idea of prohibition. What she cannot verbalize is her longing to touch Chávez as a man, as object of her desire. In a nation where woman was (is?) considered either a whore or a traitor (following the well-known formula from Monsiváis), for Teresa to express "the ecstatic feelings which tormented her," to admit that "her heart was beating in an unusual way," and that "she felt a hunger to touch him that exasperated her," would have been to lose in a single blow all the respectability and power for which she had struggled so fervently. The semantic charge of this episode announces without a doubt the imminence of Teresa's rebellion against a system that appropriated for itself the right to ascribe to Teresa an identity foreign to her. In one of her dreams, Teresa declares her displeasure to Chávez: "Oh, Cruz! I was so naive to think that maybe some day . . . but you didn't see a thing when you were here, you only wanted one thing: a saint!" (233). Domecq does not reduce her novel to a narration of the crises of others; she devotes a large part of *La insólita historia* to the fictionalization of the crisis of Teresa's very existence. She demonstrates how Teresa finally loses her "innocence and that ingenuousness with which I faced life until now" (241). The process of emancipation, however, is a laborious and intricate one, and it takes the form of a series of questions:

> What moved men to fight for lost causes with no other banner than that of her name? It was a power that went beyond her and was totally outside her control. A power that, far from healing, caused death time after time and ended up filling her with despair and guilt. (268)

> Love . . . another word that had no meaning. What was the love her friend spoke of? Had she ever loved at any time? She had fervently desired to be part of Cabora, but had she really loved that land the way Don Tomás loved it? She had emulated her father, even surpassed him, but was it for love? or was it because she wanted the power that he had? . . . When people spoke of her infinite love for the poor, had they really seen something in her or did they invent what they needed to see? (339)

Ironically, her exile to the United States and above all her arrival in the mining town of Clifton, Arizona helps her to recover part of her freedom. Out from under the burden of her renowned sainthood, she is able to verbalize and share her anguish and her love with her new friends. Nevertheless, as long as she remains near her relatives, who are the reminder of a heavy, burdensome cultural and emotional baggage, she cannot liberate herself: "She felt tired. She was twenty four years old. During the last five years she had been the instrument of Destiny and a possible participant in History, but she wanted no more. Suddenly she felt an insatiable desire to live her own life, unimportant, unnoticed, lost among so many other indistinct beings who asked only that History not make waves so they could continue a routine she had never known" (345).

Her first marriage to Guadalupe fails. She moves to San Francisco and this distance from her family allows her to find herself as a flesh and blood human being, as a person whose existence is not defined by her relationship with God and the heavens but with earth, with what is concrete, with this life and not with the promise of a life beyond. The epilogue even refers to Teresa's resurrection from (the third?) death, as though she had not renounced an "earthly" life to which she came late and which she left prematurely. While far from her family, with a person born and raised in the United States (of an American father and a Mexican mother), she succeeds in fulfilling some of her desires and accepts what she had refused for so many years: "her woman's flesh." The reader is nearly healed along with Teresa, and this is due to the fact that Domecq is able to communicate with great skill the imbalance and solitude that defined Teresa's life. She displays the personal failures that woman must survive in order to occupy a place in society. Teresa's professional development—we must not lose sight of the fact that Teresa "works"—occurs at the expense of her personal development. Her acts are constantly supervised, if not questioned. Teresa is reduced to struggling to achieve only a portion of the fullness that she seeks: "I ask myself, dear Mariana, if you are the only one in the world capable of not judging me, of accepting me just as I am, of not reinventing me either as a saint or as a devil" (373).

Domecq wants to draw the researcher and the object of her research closer together. She seeks to interpenetrate historical periods, the nineteenth and twentieth centuries, Teresa's history and experience with those of the researcher. We witness, therefore, a true osmosis between these two characters (or is it a reincarnation? (85)).

The researcher allows the rewriting of Teresa's life and the rehabilitation both of her historical memory and the memory of her being. But to the extent that Teresa's self is reconstituted, the researcher's self is also replaced, as though her investigation had a therapeutic effect. As she begins her work on Teresa, the researcher accepts "losing herself in order to become an archive of another life" (28). What she seeks to eradicate is an image of herself which, like that of Teresa, does not correspond to her: "She thinks about herself; her life is like that of a tree: a frugal existence clinging to a world foreign to her and ignores her" (41). The researcher seems disillusioned with life and she chooses to launch into the discovery of a life that will help her to redefine her own. She manifests the same desire as Teresa to reach Cabora and she makes the same pilgrimage Teresa made. She experiences a powerful erotic sensation during her encounter with nature surrounding Cabora (113). The descriptions of her emotions upon seeing her guide Javier for the first time are similar to those of Teresa for Cruz Chávez. Fiction offers Teresa and the researcher what reality withheld from them: acceptance of their body as a gendered body without giving up their professional lives. Domecq refuses to expose a body "totally imprinted by history" as destruction of the body (Butler 129–30). As Butler explains, "history is the creation of values and meanings by a signifying practice which requires the subjection of the body" (130). Thus Domecq's search for the body before the inscription that destroys it, the "pre-discursive" body (Butler 130). On the other hand, the researcher comes back to life in the same way as Teresa, with the discovery of the cave, the secret crypt, giver of life and death. The text shapes this homology by detailing the researcher's and Teresa's expressions with identical words:

> Suddenly they are there, on a small plain that opens onto the niche in the mountain, a small mouth, shallow, smiling in the rocky flank; a pink mouth, soft like the tender mouth of a calf. They crouch and enter; they can barely sit in the scarce shade; half-reclining, they rest. She observes that the floor of the cave is covered with a fine dust, the same pink color of the stone, as though it were slowly dissolving over time. She takes a little in her fingers and tastes it: it has no flavor. (149)

> Teresa took more than an hour to ascend, but finally she came to the small flat space where the cave was located. It was much smaller than it looked from a distance and she had to crouch to enter; it wasn't very deep, either, but there was some shade, and because of the height of the mountain, a breeze could reach her. . . . She looked around: the floor of the little cave was covered with a fine dust, pink in color, a product no doubt of the slow dissolving of the stone. She took some in her palm and looking toward Cabora, . . . she put some on her tongue. It had no flavor. (93–94)

Taussig asserts in another context that for some, "travelling through landscapes equals empowerment because of the meaning given them. Moving on a line in space, the traveller voyages through history, because the line gathers and joins the momentum of the power of fiction while the arrow of time pierces a motionless mosaic of space out of time, both primitive and divine" (335).

The osmosis appears likewise at the textual level in the section entitled "the fall." In it both women as subjects share the space of the written page. "The fall" alludes to two falls: Teresa's, who fell from a horse and was comatose for three months, and the researcher's, who trips on a rock as she leaves the cave. The text of the fall acts as a transition between the first two sections of *La insólita historia.* It details what "they," the researcher and Teresa, feel during their respective falls, that instant in which each had the sensation of passing between two worlds that are in reality not so different. The fall could be read as an allegory of the passage from life to death. In effect, Teresa is resurrected through the life and writing of the researcher, while part of the researcher dies to give life to Teresa. One of Teresa's anxieties, which the novel alludes to constantly, is having no one to "jump on top" of her as she used to do with others to absorb their death and so their spirit would not leave them (151). This is expressed in chapter XX, which narrates Teresa's fall. The chapter follows that which recounts the researcher's accident, and immediately precedes that of "The fall." The researcher here plays the role of absorbing death and Teresa's spirit so that she can rest in peace. What the researcher gives up in exchange for Teresa's life is that which until then was most valuable to her: her data compiled during fifteen years. She realizes that she is too implicated in the discourse she seeks to reject. This leads her to build a bridge between her professional self and her intimate, sensual self. She goes to the extreme of renouncing the empiricism of her search and the historian in her, so that the novelist can emerge, the only being capable of penetrating the spirit of Teresa and saving it from oblivion; she has privileged access to an "ontological abundance."

In synthesis, I classify *La insólita historia de la Santa de Cabora* as a "location of memory;" Domecq was able to reform memory itself through the novel. The constant play of questions about memory constitutes the text of her novel. She was able to find and be captivated by, even pierced by one of the numerous *punctum*(s) of the photographs and texts that sought to fix and write Teresa. *La insólita historia* points to the impossibility of a practice and a single epistemological coherence as long as the h/History of Teresa is still unwritten:

> You remember how this trip fascinated me because I thought I would find the answers I had always sought? I laugh at the thought

> now. In truth I found nothing, at least nothing I knew before. There are no answers. What we are is defined by life itself and only in it can we see ourselves reflected. Me? I've been a little of everything: a saint, a dreamer, a revolutionary, a visionary. What am I at the end of it all? (374)

This question also concerns the narrator of *Las púberes canéforas*, who takes on the task of exploring in a literary text the social, political and historical condemnation suffered by the homosexual population of Mexico and the problems this generates at the level of sexual gender relations and the formation of their identities.

CHAPTER 4: *LAS PÚBERES CANÉFORAS* AND THE INSCRIPTION OF SEXUAL IDENTITIES

Without a doubt, urban literary production in Mexico has experienced in the last fifteen years an appreciable and healthy growth. Healthy, for example, because it allows an artistic form such as narrative to be a forum for ideas and representations disregarded in the recent past by both social and artistic debates. Hence the fact that this type of literature favors, among other things, the emergence of a homosexual subculture.[1]

Las púberes canéforas, by Mexican writer and *cronista* (chronicler) José Joaquín Blanco, first published in 1983, is a novel that could be classified not only under the category of urban literature, but also under detective literature, protest literature, or gay literature. Despite the fascinating polysemy of this text, what is most fascinating here is that aspect of the novel which lends itself to an analysis of the inscription of homosexuality, in addition to the problems and questions which this type of inscription presents. How is the sexual identity of the main characters in this novel formed, and how is that identity lived within the urban context in which they develop? How are the dialectical tensions between the heterosexual world and the homosexual world manifested? And finally, what are the effects of the "sexualization" of social relationships between two male characters in Blanco's novel? These are a few of the questions I will seek

---

[1]There is an undeniable interest generated among Mexican readers by the theme of homosexuality: *Dos mujeres* (México, D.F.: Diana, 1990), by Sara Levi Calderón, during the spring of 1990 was fifth on the list of best sellers (Geduldig, 37). As Vicente Francisco Torres has pointed out, "narrative with gay themes in the last two decades brought us books such as *El desconocido*, (1977) and *Flash Back* (1982) by Raúl Rodríguez Cetina, *Mocambo* (1976) by Alberto Dallal; *El vino de los bravos* (1981) by Luis González de Alba; *Octavio* (1982), by Jorge Arturo Ojeda; *Sobre esta piedra* (1982), by Carlos Eduardo Turón; *Las púberes canéforas* (1983), by José Joaquín Blanco; *Utopía Gay* (1983), by José Rafael Calva; *El vampiro de la colonia Roma* (1977) and *En jirones* (1985), by Luis Zapata" (139). To this list, by no means exhaustive, we must add *Amora* by Rosamaría Roffiel and *Lunas* by Sabina Berman (México, D.F.: Editorial Katún, 1988).

to answer here. It would be ingenuous on my part, however, to suppose that this analysis provides answers which satisfy everyone. In fact, a superficial consideration of the question of sexual identity reveals the complexity surrounding the very notions of identity and sexuality, and the tendency we have of falling into reductionist and essentialist definitions. In order to embark upon the issues posed above, an examination of how Blanco's novel is organized structurally is called for first.

The first pages of *Las púberes canéforas* have the enigmatic flavor of a detective story. Who is Felipe? Who are his kidnappers and why did they kidnap him? Who is the murdered blonde woman? Immediately Felipe, a figure whose history is introduced as the center of the discursive plot, is characterized by his fear of the countryside. Thus, when his kidnappers take him to the outskirts of Mexico City, what frightens Felipe is not so much the possibility of imminent death, but rather the idea that he might die in a rural setting, in the midst of odors and noises totally strange to him: "Felipe had always lived in the city, he knew the streets and neon lights. The sensations just before his death would be unfamiliar to him" (12). Felipe does not die there, however, and the answers to the first chapter's questions begin to emerge slowly in the second chapter, thus maintaining a certain level of suspense until the end. In the second chapter he is moved from the outskirts of the city to Mexico City's Distrito Federal, the novel's central image.

The main characters are two men of different social classes separated by a generation: Felipe is eighteen and Guillermo is forty. Guillermo presents himself as gay, while Felipe, a *chichifo*[2], a "chicken" or male prostitute, seems to practice sexual acts with other men only out of economic necessity: "They had met in the streets, near a subway station in Calzada de Tlalpan, on a Saturday night; Guillermo had given him a thousand pesos" (44–45). Guillermo is narrated in third person by an "I" who is only revealed, and only for a few moments, at the end of Blanco's novel: "Suddenly Guillermo recognized me, he came over with Irene and introduced me sarcastically as a 'professional writer'" (133).

The narrative technique used here by José Joaquín Blanco allows the reader to participate in the writing and creation of the novel as he or she progresses through the reading. Not only is it the mystery woven around the enigma per se which holds the reader in suspense, but also the morphogenesis of the nov-

---

[2]Schneider explains that the word "chichifo" is "a term which, in the homosexual milieu, defines the individual who is without any absolute definitions" (85).

el. At first glance, *Las púberes canéforas* is a product of the combination of two texts. One appears scattered throughout the narration in paragraphs set off by quotation marks. Thanks to the sentences in cursive before these paragraphs, we discover that the latter are fragments which will make up "the great work, a novel that will be called *Las púberes canéforas*" (77), which Guillermo himself is writing. Some examples of the presence of a second story include: "NOTE *for Felipe as a character of the novel"* (38); MORE *notes by Guillermo on Felipe:* Felipe likes to account for everything. . ." (44); CLOTHING (*sketch*): Dress like gods. . ." (*For chapter three*)" (71). The narrator of the novel which we hold in our hands, also called *Las púberes canéforas*, includes in its textual corpus the fragments—always in quotations—of Guillermo's future novel. This technique of *mise en abyme* contributes, on the one hand, to the erasure of the boundary between narrator/narratee (Guillermo) and author (J.J. Blanco and Guillermo) in the novel(s); and on the other, to arousal of the sensation in the reader that he is in the presence of an outline of several possible versions of one novel.[3] The novel that we read can be, in this way, the product of various modes of inserting the quoted fragments and of writing. In the presence of a text far from being overdetermined, the reader is given the possibility of rearranging the pieces of this narrative puzzle and creating another novel and perhaps other identities.[4]

Formation of Sexual Identity and Urban Context: Felipe, Guillermo, La Gorda

The novel *Las púberes canéforas*, whether by Blanco, Guillermo, or both, finds its origins in the need expressed by Guillermo to tell a story that allows him to

---

[3]Upon finishing this chapter I discovered an excellent article by Jorge Ruiz Esparza on the structural composition of *Las púberes canéforas*, in which he analyzes the articulation of the concept of textuality, power, desire, and difference. Esparza does not arrive at the same conclusions as those which follow, but the two studies complement each other.

[4]For Guillermo, in the same way as for Sebastián, the narrator of the novel *En jirones* by Luis Zapata "the act of writing is not limited to recording the torturous and ultimately destructive amorous relationships with a capital A [in the case of Guillermo and Felipe]. It is principally an attempt to define, to coin a language adequate to the recording of intense emotions that are tearing him apart" (Foster 39).

tolerate his existence as a homosexual:

> Homosexual life included *long walks and long periods of loneliness*, so why not recount a novel to yourself? Why not, starting with what Felipe himself had told him, which of course would not always be true, tell yourself a story? Why not *dare to write it*? (21–22, emphasis mine)

The highlighted parts of the above quote suggest a solitary destiny, a disgraced and oppressed existence, the existence of someone who cannot reveal himself as he is without running the risk of being transformed into an anathema. The "text" is the tangible proof of his bravery, and the instance of writing is an act of resistance against the social dictum. His writing and his readings are, for him, a source of liberation, since they are what "stopped him from resigning himself to this fucking monotonous life in this city incapable of anything other than selling itself, and reselling itself fraudulently" (22). Mexico City, which Guillermo repeatedly describes, by day and by night, is a decadent, violent, corrupt city that confines homosexuality, especially that of the economic underclass, to its most dangerous and sordid places:

> Those streets which were also the refuge of poor homosexuals, in the doorways of old neighborhoods and apartment buildings where the plumbing didn't work. . . . Quick fucks in dark stairways at dawn behind broken doors, or throwing rocks to break the streetlamps, to fuck in the dark; and so many methods for sex without money, scared but enraged by your own fear: your dick hard and your lips trembling. (22)

In this novel, and in others like Luis Zapata's *El vampiro de la Colonia Roma* (*Adonis García: A Picaresque Novel*) homosexuality is represented as an effeminate occupation by virtue of its association with prostitution, a job "traditionally" performed by women, within a heterosexual context. While heterosexual prostitution—in which the object of commerce is a woman and the subject a man—is considered with each passing day more a social activity, even recognized and "necessary" in many cultures, homosexual prostitution—in which the subject and object of commerce are persons of the same sex—continues to bear the stigma of being sordid, unnatural, and irregular. It is therefore far from being raised to the level of "social function" (for good or bad) which heterosexual prostitution plays. In the field of prostitution, the homosexual occupies the place of second-class citizen and he experiences powerful discrimination. Thus the city, even in its most obscure locations, disapproves of sexual activities between persons of the same sex and tolerates them only when limited to clandestine bars and the most dangerous streets of the metropolis. While at the same time condemning homosexuality, there are many "Christians," kinetic instruments of what Judith Butler calls the "heterosexual matrix" (*Gender Trouble* xi), who promote homosexual prostitution, labelling its participants as prisoners of their own trap who cannot assert socially or diurnally their sexual "desires": "That respectable family man, for example, who on an escapade after a few drinks during an anniversary celebration or an office party hired a chichifo" (76). Throughout the novel the role and function of the "chicken" is emphasized in a society where the erotic ethos is defined according to social and moral norms traditionally bound to the "patriarchal Manichaeist paradigm," a society for which "this conception of gender presupposes not only a causal relation among sex, gender, and desire, but suggests as well that desire reflects or expresses gender and that gender reflects or expresses desire" (Butler 1990; 22).

As was mentioned at the beginning of this chapter, *Las púberes canéforas* presents a spectrum of male characters seeking to give meaning to their lives. Though here the principal "body" on which the Mexican erotic ethos is inscribed is the gay male body, I propose that this body cannot be defined unilaterally as homosexual. The sexual identity of the different male "bodies"—if such an identification is possible—is formed in each case, despite their common denominators, in a distinct fashion.

Felipe is paradigmatic of many young people, male and female, who come to the city with hopes of a life better than that which their home villages can offer them. Their first contact with the metropolis demythologizes the city, because opportunities are rare and work is a chimera. Felipe only adds to the total number of already numerous delinquents in the urban jungle. Felipe is led into prostitution, according to Guillermo's story, by his desire to have access to the consumer world. Mexico City offers him a new semiotic universe where the codes of language and relationships have been transformed dramatically. The young man responds to these new signs and messages exactly as their creators had foreseen: "He was dazzled by the city and he left his studies in favor of movies, Finnish jackets, tape players, parties in pseudopalatial condominiums, cars, motorcycles, and with luck even a trip to Acapulco" (44). He is fascinated by the new myths, by the worldly success that takes so little effort. Guillermo fictionalizes a character whose self is limited to a void sign, "colonized from within by technologies for immune bodies, a virtual technology mediated by designer bodies subjected to automated image systems" (Kroker and Cook 8).

The city in *Las púberes canéforas* and in the majority of recent urban novels operates as "the ideal locus for the late capitalist consumer machine and is established by its political economy of signs . . . which covers the surface of the body with its tattoo like a text, staging at the same time the article of consumption as a source of power" (Kroker and Cook 17). Felipe's life is regulated to a large extent by these signs of fashion, and he chooses to move into Guillermo's apartment, since the latter offers Felipe financial help in exchange for sexual favors.

Felipe is one of the most successful characters of this novel and perhaps of many urban novels which include the theme of homosexuality, in spite of some ambiguities surrounding him which we will turn to later by way of conclusion. In effect, he resists any kind of gender definition formulated on the basis of his sexual activity, his sex, or his desire. He fascinates everyone: "Irene fell instantly in love with Felipe. Everyone, drunk or half drunk, transvestite or body builder, fem or butch, in drag or maintaining the conventional bearing of office decency, they all observed his appearance with some shock" (141). Felipe is a "chichifo" because he chooses the male gender (whether heterosexual or homosexual) as the object of his trade. This alone is not sufficient, however, to define him as homosexual, as various factors can explain his choice. In the first place, "heterosexual" prostitution, as so defined, would imply that Felipe sells his body to a woman in exchange for money paid by her, which would make of him a kept man and could, within a Hispanic cultural context, signify either little or great manliness. Furthermore, prostitution limited to sexual exchanges between persons of the same sex, more specifically here between "males," can be more lucrative as a result of the social censure around homosexuality or simply around sexual activity between persons of the same sex. Finally, the object of Felipe's desire is located in a person of his own sex, a fact which does not necessarily identify him as a homosexual.[5] Moreover, his relationship with Analía confirms that Felipe's eroticism is not concentrated solely on the male gender, and that gender and desire do not converge systematically.

As Eve Sedgwick explains in her lucid and valuable study *Epistemology of the Closet*, "modern Western culture has placed what it calls sexuality in a more and more distinctively privileged relation with our most prized constructions of individual identity, truth and knowledge" (3). The sexual/genital activity of Felipe does not permit pigeonholing him from a gender point of view. This

---

[5]In popular Latin American culture the one who is penetrated is the homosexual. The one who penetrates is fulfilling the traditional role that God gave him at birth. As long as he penetrates he is not stigmatized to such an extent; but if he is penetrated, he loses all respect from Latin American "machos."

activity, on the other hand, does allow him access to the market economy and thus permits him to take up the process of social identification. The sexual act and the object of his desire do not determine Felipe's gender, nor does he wish to see himself circumscribed by his sexuality: "Both Felipe and Analía were astonished that sex was so important to people: so dramatic, so deforming; that people could be so weak, so desirous, so enslaved by excessive appetites" (73).

Guillermo, on the other hand, embodies the civil servant impassioned by writing, a divorced man who "declares" himself homosexual. His relationship with Felipe underlines the difference between the two. For Guillermo, sexuality regulates both his mental and emotional life. Not only does he become totally dependent (especially sexually dependent on Felipe), but this "addiction" causes him, moreover, anxiety and rage when he realizes that his desire for Felipe gives the latter complete superiority and control in the relationship. What he refuses to forgive Felipe is his youth, this being reflected in his physical makeup, which Felipe exploits to the extreme: "this urban prostitution, for example, Guillermo thought, slave to unsatisfiable industrial sensualities, to the type of industrial Apollo embodied in fashion models and the Olympus drawn from television commercials" (39). This quote obviously feeds the critical-social discourse which permeates the entire novel, but it is also representative of Guillermo's desperation. To relieve the disgust overtaking him day by day, he finds an escape valve, a way of consoling himself from the humiliation and pain that Felipe inflicts upon him: the power that writing gives him. While Felipe controls Guillermo's sexuality, the latter has authority over the literary creation of Felipe's identity, and "vengeful, Guillermo translated the young man into a disparaging language of coarse mercantile comparisons" (39). This refuge, however, does not prevent him from admitting that he desires "now that youth has past, that ideal of homosexual coitus like an encounter of demigod basketball players displaying first-class muscles" (40).

La Gorda is of particular interest: "La Gorda was not really fat as such; on the contrary, he was short, strong and thin, with a thick, stiff moustache like a Zapatista revolutionary soldier in the Casola Archives. . . . He didn't let his body go to pot. Forty years old" (54). La Gorda's peculiarity rests on the fact that he is the only character to speak freely about how his first sexual desires were manifested. In his speech, La Gorda seems to indicate that his desire for persons of the same sex always dominated his erotic life: "But ever since I was a little boy Indian men fascinated me. One is such a whore from birth, right?" (57). His attraction to Indians, laborers and peasants results more from the censure imposed by his social class. For La Gorda, laborers symbolized otherness, difference, and at the same time, the natural, freedom, everything opposed to the rules, norms, and virtues dictated by his family and social decorum. The bodies of laborers, the only half nude bodies offered to his view, awake in La Gorda carnal desire and sensuality, and they are transformed into the object of his sexual fantasies. Though questions of an "ontogenic" and "philogenic" order are of no importance to La Gorda, he delights in mentioning that his parents always mistakenly, like the rest of society, perceived homosexuality as a phenomenon of sexual metastasis.[6] If homosexuality is the result of an inversion phenomenon, it is then a "controllable" phenomenon, or at least something that can be prevented if the individual's environment contains the necessary conditions:

> I would get so bored. I would ask my dad to send me out with his laborers to entertain myself, and he would say yes; because, between my mom, her friends, grandmother, my aunts, the church and everything else, not to mention the house where you couldn't be in any room without hearing soap operas on TV or radio . . . I was going to turn into a fag (my dad used to say), and among working-class machos I was going to turn into a little man. It was exactly the opposite, who would have said it, huh? and my brothers, who were the biggest hypocrites, now you see them as model fathers, local entrepreneurs. . . . And I, who was always the strongest, from so many sports and fights, turned out to be a little fairy. . . . (59-60).

La Gorda seeks to destabilize assumptions given as eternal truths, to shatter the concept of homosexuality and sexuality as a binary system through humor, and he demonstrates that "the construction of a coherent sexual identity along the disjunctive axis of the feminine/masculine axis is bound to fail" (Butler, *Gender Trouble* 28). Nevertheless, he lives a social and professional existence as a "closet" homosexual: "He always attracted bourgeois mothers with his healthy and youthful looks, his tight waist and his thick forearms" (64).

From the above, it seems that one of the common factors in the formation of Felipe's, Guillermo's, and La Gorda's identities is an obsession with staying young. A preoccupation with age, with physical decrepitude, is ever present in this novel. This is a traditionally feminine concern, or more appropri-

---

[6]Eve Sedgwick, in her study *Epistemology of the Closet*, reflects critically on the notions of philogeny and ontogeny, defining them as reductive notions which force whoever takes up the task of explaining homosexuality to adopt an essentialist position; cf. 40–42.

ately the lot of women, whose bodies after a certain age are no longer, in many cultures, attractive and thus are much less accepted when matched with the youthful body of their male counterpart. Guillermo takes great care to remain in good physical condition in order to "please," an attitude adjudicated to the female gender in heterosexual relationships, while this kind of demand is not usually applied to the (heterosexual) male with the same amount of pressure: "The less attention I pay to my physical condition, the more masculine I will be" (Monsiváis; *Escenas*; 116). Guillermo defines himself as a homosexual—although in the closet—but this condition is circumscribed to a homosexuality understood in Foucauldian terms as a "gender inversion and gender transitivity" (Sedgwick 1985; 45-46). This is surprising, since the homosexuality that marks and traverses the story associates itself more with "the virility of the homosexual orientation of male desire [which] seemed as self-evident to the ancient Spartans, and . . . (not merely of "the feminine", but of actual women as well)." (Sedgwick 1985; 27). An interesting displacement is then produced: age becomes an important element in the process of identity formation for these three characters; it becomes more transcendent than the problem of sexuality or of gender, though these two problems run parallel through the entire text. Blanco devotes a large part of the novel to some of the new manifestations of male eroticism in the Distrito Federal, in which the important thing is a stereotyped body shape which can guarantee, with good physical conditions, any kind of success:

> So many people passionately subjected to their adolescent fantasies, embodying them into their old age with an excessive obsession: the entire virile apogee of comic books, Tarzan and Kaliman bodies, in which goodness and success were defined by the number of muscular bulges, the powerful triangulation of the thorax with a narrow waist above abundant virile buttocks and a tiny loincloth, adequately bulging in front, that combined with adorable faces like plastic dolls—straight noses, long eyelashes, perfect symmetry—and powerful bronze gladiator legs. (131)

The bodybuilding which most of the male characters practice functions here as an architectural trope, especially when associated with the bodybuilding practiced by young men who have sexual relationships with other men. This architectural trope symbolizes the osmosis between the human body and the urban material body, each dependent on the other. Felipe, for example, is determined to shape and maintain his body in the image of the glass skyscrapers of the wealthy Paseo de la Reforma, the only avenue with which he desires to identify: "Towers of crystal, of ice, almost of light. Certain buildings on the Paseo de la Reforma drive him crazy, like mirrors that reflect other mirrored buildings which in turn. . ." (45). He sees his silhouette as a human replica of the materially successful and the physically modern, a replica of structural expression of the architectural and the urban. His hope or dream is to be able one day to harmonize with this urban environment, to feel himself in total symbiosis with the glass buildings reflecting their "morphology" in Felipe's glistening muscles, while Felipe's image bounces on the refracting windows. This reflection never goes beyond a morphological construction, or the space of a pictorial representation. Felipe only identifies with the apparently healthy framework of La Reforma, with hyperreality, thus reducing the inscription of his self in this microcosm of Mexico City to a material inscription.

Though Guillermo and La Gorda also devote themselves to the cult of the body to keep themselves attractive and sexually "alive," they are aware of the deceit this embodies and they realize, as Lefebvre says, that in this instance "sports and exercise are nothing more than parodies, simulations of the culture of the body" (193). The city which Guillermo moves through is drastically opposite the regular constructions of La Reforma which Felipe personifies: Guillermo's city, like Guillermo himself, carries within the novel a "rhetoric of disturbance."[7] This rhetoric is made patent in the descriptions of other *loci*, such as Insurgente Norte, Eje 2 Norte, or Avenida Manuel González, where Guillermo sees crumbling bridges, collapsed houses, run-down automobiles, or partially completed structures as he "walks." Guillermo's tale of the decrepit train station (once the pride of Mexico and the symbol of progress) here displays only signs of decay. The ruined or half-finished structures could also be the result of earthquakes; they remain, however, as iconic displays of the failures of sixties urbanization. Guillermo's and Felipe's readings of the city differ powerfully, which could be the result of a generational conflict. The mimetic relationship between the decayed urban whole described by Guillermo and the effects of age that he admits to bearing himself echo his anguish over physical senility. He realizes that he is already greatly disadvantaged with respect to what he calls "the industrial Apollo" and the "individualist capital" that represents the Apollo's appearance:

> For some time Guillermo and La Gorda had gotten into the habit of feeling old; partly because the people who moved publicly through the

---

[7]I borrow this formula from the theoretical vocabulary of the architectural field, and more specifically from critic Judith Wolin (23).

> more or less homosexual parts of the city were usually very young (who after a few years of sex and partying left disillusioned or pressured by social forces; they married and accepted normal lives, or they simply closed themselves in their private existences). (56)

When they feel crushed by the world around them, Guillermo and La Gorda advocate the return to a vision of sexuality in which desire is not "industrialized, packaged and canned in the business of making profits with it" (151). They both long for a lost space equivalent here to the rural setting and its culture, where sex is presented for them as something "natural," outside the mercantile, where one has no reason to be a "mattress superman:" "We should be more modest about sex, like in the peasant cultures, more natural; the same with feelings . . . take that excessively urban attribute of vital luxury away from sex" (41). La Gorda reiterates this type of polarization between the urban-artificial and the rural-natural, idealizing the countryside and fantasizing a sexual encounter with the "noble savage," the Indian. As he admits, it is only a fantasy, and a racist one besides. He recognizes that the "native" cannot be reduced to the natural and benevolent, and that his desire for a "prehistoric" sexuality, for a "subverted" Eden, is a dream not only utopian, but also counterproductive.

Beginning with chapter five, we discover a series of characters whose identities and sexualities are formed differently from the three previously mentioned.

Dialectical Tensions between the Heterosexual and Homosexual Worlds and the Sexualization of Sexual Relationships

Other characters appear in the story and their cases also present interesting peculiarities, as is the case with Ignacio and Fabian. The two are friends, but Fabian is entirely unaware of Ignacio's sexual activities. Fabian works in a factory (Fábrica Clincson, S.A.), Ignacio is a student in preparatory school and hopes to be a physicist. The two are tied to the other characters by virtue of their also being victims of the "guaruras" or "johns", the male prostitution customers who assaulted Felipe, and also because of the sexual relationship between Ignacio and La Gorda: "Ignacio worked as a male prostitute from time to time, he said it was only to make his expenses, because at home they couldn't help him much" (112). For Ignacio, unlike Felipe, sexual relationships with persons of his own sex come to mean more than a simple means of sustenance. When he decides to leave prostitution behind, he cannot end his relationship with La Gorda because he experiences the sexual encounter with him as a real source of pleasure. He will only leave La Gorda when he finds in Fabian something more than a drinking and partying "cuate" or buddy.[8] During one of their Sunday outings, returning to the city from the Balneario Los Pelicanos, where Fabian and Ignacio went often, the revelation occurs. As they travel, it occurs to Ignacio momentarily that Fabian is making advances toward him: "Ignacio thought that, lightheaded from the booze, Fabian was trying to pick him up. It would be entertaining: an adventure where he least expected it, with whom he least imagined it possible" (116). Ignacio, however, tries to elude these displays for two reasons: in the first place because by opening himself to Fabian "he would get burned in his neighborhood and those things always got out" (116).[9] In other words, his greatest concern is to keep his sexual desire hidden; and secondly, because he prefers to lose the possible one-night stand rather than a friend, and moreover he later "would feel remorse and would try to start a fight with him to relieve his guilt" (116). Upon arriving at Cuautla, Fabian suggests to Ignacio, who would have preferred to return to Mexico City as soon as possible, that they take the early morning bus to the city instead and take a room in the hotel near the bus station. Once in the hotel, Fabian slips into Ignacio's bed and they make love. Fabian asks him: "Is

---

[8]See the excellent study by Larissa Adler de Lomnitz on the phenomenon of "cuatismo."

[9]The idea of "opening oneself up" referred to in Ignacio's text is one which Octavio Paz linked, in the fifties in *The Labyrinth of Solitude*, with the idea of "cracking" as a form of abdication: "Our relationships with other men are always tinged with suspicion. Every time a Mexican confides in a friend or acquaintance, every time he opens himself up, it is an abdication. He dreads that the person in whom he has confided will scorn him. . . . Our anger is prompted not only by the fear of being used by our confidants—that fear is common to everyone—but also by the shame of having renounced our solitude. . . . The Mexican macho—the male—is a hermetic being, closed up in himself. . ." (30–31, 54). J. J. Blanco's text, however, is presented as an attempt at overcoming the definition in which relationships between Mexicans—whether social or sexual—have been enclosed. It attempts to escape that solitude, that comfortable situation behind which the Mexican male withdraws in order not to confront the reality around him, and to erase the negative nexus between "opening up" and "cracking," to give place instead to the positive nexus between "opening up" and "freeing" oneself. Accepting, at the end of the twentieth century, the idea of "opening up" as a synonym of "cracking", would be equivalent to preserving the patriarchal hegemonic system within which these concepts were created.

this the first time you've fucked a man? Or about the same as the first time. . . Oh, you rascal . . . Fabian laughed" (121). Ignacio is surprised that Fabian, about to marry Margarita, reacts so simply and naturally to this relationship. In reality, however, the sexual act with Ignacio for Fabian only represents another element of "cuatismo," a component of the bonds of friendship among males: "They talked, embracing, in Ignacio's bed. They had promised to be like brothers to each other, but "fucking brothers." The thing about Margarita was separate: women were one mess, "cuates" were another very different one, right?" (121). Not only does the semantically loaded expressions and words such as "fucking men," "brothers" but also the opposition between the "cuates" and "women are one mess" contributes to the virilization of the situation, and they point out Fabian's intention that his commitment to Ignacio be limited to a "homosocial" relationship. In other words, Fabian, considering his sexual activity with Ignacio as a logical extension of "cuatismo" and limiting it to the concept of brotherhood, denies the notion of desire and the "potentially erotic," and he rejects the possibility of a "continuum between the homosocial and the homosexual" (Sedgwick 1985; 2). If there is a continuum (I think there is), Fabian would prefer not to mention it. By choosing not to name it, he "admits vulnerability in the need for naming" (Spivak in Koundoura 86). The "diacritical opposition" between the "homosocial" and the "homosexual" which Fabian uses is his way of legitimating his desire. Homosociality is the mask he chooses to cover himself with in order not to confront social censure. This subterfuge prevents the reaction which Ignacio expects of Fabian: one of violence to "relieve his guilt." On the contrary, the "guaruras" and other men who search in secrecy for same-sex erotic encounters compensate for their moment of "weakness" with violence. They become enraged and they humiliate or strike and injure the sexual object in the person of the "chichifo," who recalls their own indecency, the worst which they believe they carry inside of them.[10] The mask behind which they carry out their pretense is that of homophobia: the sexual act with the "other" of the same sex finds justification as long as it is carried out under the sign of degradation and hatred, in reality a hatred of themselves.

Sedgwick, in another of her informative studies on homosocial desire, explains that "obligatory heterosexuality is built into male-dominated kinship

[10]Throughout the novel, the idea of "penetration" is almost never alluded to. This may suggest that the author sought to erase the implicit and problematic opposition between the penetrator and the penetrated by which sexual identity is traditionally defined.

systems, or that homophobia is a necessary consequence of such patriarchal institutions as heterosexual marriage" (1985; 3). The impulse of these characters limiting desire for a person of the same sex to the homosocial (at the same time denying the sexual "continuum") and linking violence with the "homosexual" genital act is paradigmatic of the difficulty they all have of "coming out" and "accepting" themselves sexually. They are imprisoned in a system of definitions and predeterminations established by a society entrenched in Catholicism, which promotes the supremacy of the strong, virile man in the service of biological reproduction and progress. This is a supremacy of what Rorty calls "the social engineer." It turns out, however, that our "social engineer" is the product of patriarchal engineering, synonymous here with circular labor, the opposite of progress by the definition of that very same engineering (Spivak, as quoted by Koundoura 89).

Likewise, the relationships maintained by Fabian and Felipe with their female counterparts are obviously another product of the hegemonic system. Felipe decides to break up with Guillermo to live with Analía. The story of Felipe's feelings for Analía, however, is somewhat ambiguous:

> Felipe was rich because that morning he had sold the quadraphonic, and he was feeling lavish and generous enough to invite Analía, like a real lady, out for a night of extravagance. Just to arrive with her, so attractive and serious, a seriousness that gave her even more elegance, made him feel more distinguished himself, closer to success, more capable and more secure. (79)

In various places in the text, the narrator mentions Felipe's pride when being with Analía and insists on how serious she is. He does not mention Analía as a loved one, however, but rather as some one who "made him [Felipe] feel more distinguished himself." He sees her as another piece of furniture, though necessary in his life, as a "provider" of the social respectability that he yearns for.

Fabian completely hides, as expected, both his homosocial and his homosexual relationships from Margarita ("women are one mess"). Both Fabian and Felipe, however, are conscious of the social and economic importance (according to the patriarchal hegemonic system) which women bear:

> Ignacio should find a girl already. . . . That way the four of them could go on vacation, to the movies, dancing, like a family, right? And even get a decent apartment for the four, with four salaries: each couple their

own bedroom and share the rest: instead of shacking up with fucking relatives: better off setting up house like two blood brothers. (121)

Fabian not only considers Margarita and Ignacio's future partner as sources of income, but also—and perhaps more importantly—as legitimating elements of his domestic felicity with Ignacio. While Fabian rejects "social" identification, that is, a public identification with homosexuality, he nevertheless has difficulty completely denying the object of his desire. As he becomes aware of his physical and emotional attraction toward Ignacio—without accepting as a consequence the continuum between the homosocial and the homosexual—he decides to find a way to live with him. Women thus become victims of the commodification in which Fabian finds himself "obligated" to enclose them. The "cuatismo" between Fabian and Ignacio masks inhibition and repression or perhaps sublimation, but it nevertheless remains dependent on misogynous machismo in order to exist.

The solution which Fabian proposes is the one which his narrator and creator Guillermo invents and idealizes. Guillermo seeks to inscribe his own desire on Fabian and Ignacio, his longing to see a day when homosexual couples live out their love with the same civil rights as heterosexuals. The interesting thing, however, is that Guillermo self-censors his writing, convinced that daily reality and perhaps the very world of literary production and publication implicitly forbid him the possibility of fictionalizing his desire and his hopes; Fabian is injured (presumably fatally) during the Fábrica Clincson strike, and Guillermo writes: "Ignacio and Fabian: two unreal figures, of course unbelievable in their love story" (121). With this Fabian and Ignacio find themselves "amputated from the literary text."

In the Mexican urban context presented in *Las púberes canéforas*, homosexuality is far from forming part of the "public sphere." The only truly public manifestation of homosexuality in the novel, besides prostitution, is the "Drag Queen 82 and Mr. Gay Hercules J" contest, in which members of the heterosexual community participate as spectators. This contest is made up of a bodybuilder's competition, a runway lottery of nude "chichifos" and a transvestite's competition. We will now turn to this last aspect of the contest.

In her essay on the film *Paris is Burning*, Judith Butler (1993) correctly points out the complexity of the concept and practice of drag. There is no doubt that for the transvestite this act of "transformation" and "disguise" implies much more than a mere act of parodying the reigning norms. For the (uninformed) heterosexual spectator, the concept of drag is read generally, as an act of parody which, strangely, is not as alienating as it would seem. Hence the fact that Butler questions the practice of drag per se as a subversive act. She proposes that this type of "denaturalization of gender could be the same vehicle towards the reconsolidation of hegemonic forms" (*Bodies That Matter* 125). She adds that "drag could be, in reality, in the service both of denaturalization and of reidealization of hyperbolic heterosexual gender norms" (*Bodies That Matter* 125). Starting from this declaration, I propose that the contest episode highlights precisely the idea of "reidealization." In fact, each transvestite impersonates a woman like Joan Crawford, María Felix, Lola Beltrán; moreover, the winner of the contest is always the same, "a shoe store owner who each year appears in a different impersonation of María Felix" (135).

Monsiváis and other critics have analyzed the "mythic condition" of María Félix which "is grounded in her enduring beauty" ("Las mitologías" 18). What separates Félix from her contemporaries like Dolores del Río, however, is the fact that, according to Monsiváis, she was a "woman in charge of her own destiny . . . and that she instilled in her characters the dictates of her own personality, the luxury that beauty demands, the voice hoarse in an incessant act of commanding" (18). In other words, Félix is a character who seduces and who is converted into fantasy for both the heterosexual female viewer who wants to *be* Félix, and for the heterosexual male viewer who is helplessly fascinated by women like Félix as long as they remain on the screen, dominating him from a distance without becoming a daily reality. Thus the kind of cross-dressing presented and rewarded here is reduced to a "reiterative production" of a femininity established and accepted as national myth, a myth which the transvestite renews, recreates, and "reidealizes" year after year. There is no doubt that the drag queens and supermasculinized gay hercules are here represented according to the cultural criteria established by ancient as well as more recent national heterosexual "institutions." In this way, the entrance of La Gorda and the other gay characters into the public sphere is only possible as long as their subversive act is approved by the public and stays within the limits representing the geography of the spectacle. Thus, drag becomes equivalent here to an "impersonation of the hegemonic norms" which Butler referred to previously. The stage, the gulf dividing the world of those who view and those who are viewed, permits the public's participation with these characters; without the comic-grotesque aspect surrounding the spectacle for the viewer, the heterosexual/homosexual encounter would not be possible.

The world of homosexuality is synonymous here with the nocturnal, the clandestine, the spectacle, with sordid violence and the underworld. But for La Gorda, it is better to exist in these conditions than not to be able to exist at all. For him/her, ironically, the homosexual's lot is closely linked with the police:

"The little that we have achieved is thanks to the police and to corruption. The spaces in which we can move and breathe more or less, haven't been given us by the Ladies of St. Vincent or the Knights of Columbus or the House of Representatives, but by the police" (146). La Gorda decides, in spite of everything, not to pay the extortsion money that two policemen demand as he leaves the Jáuregui Baths for having had sex with minors in the baths. Nor does he take out the false police credentials which could frighten away the officers. He prefers to suffer their humiliations and blows rather than continue in silence and secrecy about his homosexuality. By rebelling, he publicly articulates his desire to discover himself just as he is. Tired of the deceit of a diurnal public self antagonistically opposed to a nocturnal public self, both likewise foreign to what the private self wishes for its true self, La Gorda, in a moment of daring and courage, crosses the threshold of the forbidden and comes out.

Of all the identities that this novel attempts to form, La Gorda's is the least ambiguous. The ambiguity surrounding the identity of Felipe or of Ignacio, for example, is somewhat problematic. In effect, the underlying message that can be read through the formation of their sexual identity insinuates that they surrender to the "genital homosexual" act for economic reasons. Society judges this state of action as the product of a "circumstantial" situation, "incidental" and therefore it is disposed toward "indulgence." Homosexuality is "tolerated" then because it is possible to rationalize the attitude of those who have chosen a different "eros" from the majority. As long as homosexuality can be associated with an "explanation" (in this case the economic situation) and the participant and his actions associated with the space in which he acts, homophobic society feels sheltered, annihilating the very concept of difference, but "without having freed itself thereby from the idea of difference" (Butler, *Gender Trouble* 112). When homosexuality is defined as a circumstantial phenomenon it is controllable. Knowing whether the young homosexual male falls into the world of prostitution because this is the only sphere in which he can express both his sexual and social identities matters very little. This vicious circle makes a relationship like Fabian's and Ignacio's impossible even in the world of fiction.

Judith Butler proves convincingly that "multiple and coexisting identifications produce conflicts, convergences and innovative dissonances within gender configurations which contest the fixity of masculine and feminine placements with respect to the paternal law" (*Gender Trouble* 67). The success of this novel lies precisely in having fictionalized characters without a fixed sexual identity, characters whose genders do not determine systematically their respective sexual identities. Felipe accepts the modality of desire embodied by his client and he satisfies this desire. At the same time, the modality of Felipe's object and desire are also located in the binary gender system in which desire must be "oppositional." He oscillates between various modalities. Fabian, on the other hand, presents himself as a "heterosexual" for whom the modality and the object of homosexual desire are thinkable only in terms of "cuatismo" and of homosociality. He maintains sexual relations with Ignacio and with Margarita. Guillermo and La Gorda are the characters who most explicitly destabilize the gender identity established according to the desire for an object of the opposite sex. They escape, each in his own way, the definition of gender imposed by the Patriarchal Law; this is not accomplished, however, without risks and can even cost them their lives.[11]

In this novel José Joaquín Blanco tries to avoid enclosing his characters indifferently in the single—segregationist—categoryof homosexuality, and he invites instead a vision of homosexuality that is more pluralistic and polymorphous.

These questions also concerned another Mexican writer in the fifties, Miguel Barbachano Ponce. In his novel *El diario de José Toledo*, Barbachano Ponce fictionalizes one of the problems which *Las púberes canéforas* poses: that of misogynous machismo and what this attitudes entails for the man whose intimate female psychic space finds itself a prisoner in a male body.

---

[11]It is important to note that for a novel written in 1983, when the idea of exchange of "bodily fluids" is very much in the public eye, the failure to make mention of the AIDS dilemma is surprising. This silence about the problem could be a manifestation of the different concerns that Mexican gay writers have with respect to their Western and especially North American counterparts. It could also be that the Distrito Federal of Mexico in 1983 had not yet entered the age of "panic sex" in which many other Western urban centers were living. Or is it that Blanco simply refused to associate homosexuality, already socially condemned, with the stigma of the deadly infection?

CHAPTER 5: *EL DIARIO DE JOSÉ TOLEDO*: A QUEER SPACE IN THE WORLD OF MEXICAN LETTERS

Judging from the homophobic response in 1991 disclosed by Mexican national state officials to a gay conference to be held in Guadalajara, such Mexican gay and lesbian groups as GOHL (Grupo Orgullo de Liberación Homosexual [Homosexual Liberation Pride Group]), Colectivo Sol (Sun Collective), Gay Guerrilla, Grupo Homosexual de Acción Revolucionario (Homosexual Revolutionary Action Group), and Grupo Lésbico Patlatonalli (Lesbian Group Patlatonalli)[1] still have a long way to go. This said, Mexico is also one of the first countries in Latin America to "decriminalize" homosexuality, and it boasts perhaps the longest history of gay and lesbian activism, as outlined by Matthews:

> In the midseventies, a gay men's discussion group emerged at the Autonomous Metropolitan University (UNAM). Its members went on to found the first gay militant group, the Homosexual Front for Revolutionary Action (FHAR). Other groups, such as the lesbian Oikabeth and cosexual Lambda emerged soon after. By the late seventies, Mexico City had its first gay pride day march. (58)[2]

Since the late seventies, Mexico City has been the site of many gay and lesbian pride marches. Numerous cultural and artistic events have also taken place in support of homosexual liberation. One of the most significant events was the creation of Semana Cultural Gay (Gay Cultural Week) in June of 1982 whose

---

[1]The meaning that this group gives to the word "Patlatonalli" is unclear. The word does not appear in the Diccionario de la lengua nahuatl o mexicana by Rémi Siméon. The words *patla* and *tonalli* do appear individually, however. The first word means 1) to become bored, to tire of waiting, to despair, to distrust; 2) to replace one person with another; 3) to change, to exchange, trade, or melt an object (376). The definitions of *tonalli* are: 1) heat, heat of the sun, summer; 2) soul, spirit, birth sign.

[2]The first march of a gay and lesbian group took place on July 26 of 1978 in Mexico City during the commemoration of the 1968 student movement.

slogan was "we are everywhere." Semana Cultural Gay occurred every year, with the exception of 1983. Today it provides a space for cultural and artistic expression of Mexican gay and lesbian communities as well as for individuals and organisations–whether social, political, or professional. Moreover, this event brings together people who are eager to share their views, ideas, and concerns, or simply to cooperate and work with gays and lesbians as full members of society.[3] The Universidad Nacional de México, and the Círculo Cultural Gay (Gay Cultural Circle) organize these events, and the Museo Universitario del Chopo has hosted them since 1987. These organized events not only give the community a sense of continuity, but also a sense of "affiliation" with more institutionalized sectors of Mexican society. Of course, the notion of decriminalization alluded to earlier is relative. The nineties, for example, are witnessing a retrogression of social and political activism in defense of homosexuals' rights. Ian Lumsden's study of homosexuality in Mexico gives an account of the territory being lost by different gay communities: the initial enthusiam that led to the creation of reviews and periodicals such as *Nuestro cuerpo*, formed by FHAR, and *Nuevo ambiente*, created by Lambda, or the formation of gay organizations or clubs and their mobilization and participation in celebrations such as Gay Pride Day (72–73), is slowly diminishing. Nevertheless, even though the political parties, including those of the left like the PRT (Partido Revolucionario de Trabajadores, Revolutionary Workers' Party) refuse now more than ever to raise the flag of defense for homosexual groups (in the 1982 elections the PRT supported such actions), Lumsden adds that

> *Televisa*, the most important television network in Mexico, which has always been sexist and politically reactionary, recently changed substantially its way of presenting news related to homosexuality and to AIDS. This is as significant as the favorable attitude toward gays in newspapers and journals of smaller circulation such as *La Jornada*,

---

[3]For a history of Semana Cultural Gay, see Carlos Blas Galindo's article "Cultura artística y homosexualidad." Galindo is a cultural critic and artist specializing in visual arts, and he was one of the first to denounce the censorship surrounding the Semana Cultural Gay in 1989; see his "Censura en el Museo del Chopo" and "Reseña de una censura negada," both in his *Ex profeso*.

> *El Nacional*, and *Proceso*, since television is by far the most popular communication medium. (75)[4]

Carlos Blas Galindo, a fervent defender of gay and lesbian artistic expression, reminds us that in Mexico "the first groups to engage in the battle for homosexual liberation were essentially made up of intellectuals, artists, and students" (16; my translation), who were later joined by more radical political and social groups. The field of literature in Mexico has been particularly propitious to the dissemination of the themes of homosexuality and to the inscription of gay and lesbian sensibilities in aesthetic terms.[5]

El diario de José Toledo (*José Toledo's Diary*, 1964) by Miguel Barbachano Ponce is paradigmatic of the inscription of homosexuality in the aesthetic category of literature. The study of this novel opens at least two lines of investigation that I propose to examine here. The first deals with various textual strategies which Barbachano Ponce deploys in order to debunk and erode the precognitive literary and social foundations on which more traditional literary texts are erected. The second issue deals with the narrativization of homosexuality in Mexico in the 1950s. I then examine the ontological and epistemic choices posed by the novel and the ideological and political implications this fictional discourse had within the specific sociohistorical context of its production.

Barbachano Ponce wrote his first novel in the midst of a literary euphoria. Indeed, the 1960s marked a healthy break with traditional Mexican literary production. Authors like José Agustín and Gustavo Sainz initiated an imaginative and defiant narrative, shaping a provocatively new language inspired by their surrounding reality. These constantly transforming narrative techniques strived

---

[4]Lumsden provides a very exhaustive analysis of the gay liberation movements in Mexico and their evolution in chapters five and six. His bibliography contains especially valuable references; for example, he refers to the works of Gina Fratti and Adriana Batista, Liberación Homosexual (1984); Juan Jacobo Hernández and Rafael Manrique, "10 años del movimiento gay en Mexico," *La guillotina* 16 (September 1988); Jaime Leroux, "El MHL más allá del desgreñe," *La guillotina* 17 (March 1989); Colectivo Masiosare, "Tolerancia y democracia en el MHL," *La guillotina* 17 (March 1989); Juan Carlos Batista, "El fin de la democracia gay," *Nexos* 139 (July 1989).

[5]*Latin American Gay and Lesbian Writing: A Bio-Bibliographical Sourcebook*, edited by David William Foster, offers a good number of entries on Mexican literature.

to translate contemporary social and political preoccupations and commitments. They also hoped to convey the diversity which shaped urban Mexican society and culture (cf. Poniatowska 167–206). *El diario de José Toledo,* which earned recognition as the first novel in Mexico to openly inscribe homosexuality in literature (Schneider 82), could not have come out, so to speak, at a better moment. Yet however timely his statement was in 1964, Barbachano Ponce failed to find a publisher for his novel. Far from balking at defeat, he resolved to publish it at his own expense. Twenty-four years went by before the publishing house Premiá reprinted his novel in 1988. Today, to find *El diario de José Toledo* in a bookstore—even in Mexico City—remains an arduous undertaking. What explains the meager dissemination—past and present—of this publication and the leaden silence encompassing it?

The 1960s in Mexico proved to be liberating only for a few. Barbachano Ponce did not benefit from the magnanimity of Mexican readers. In a recent conversation, the author acknowledged that the publication of this novel considerably hindered his carreer as a writer. This adversity was clearly a result of the censorship imposed by homophobia. He confronted his marginalization in the world of Mexican letters. Barbachano Ponce attributes the negative reception of his work to the closemindedness of the Mexican literary establishment of the time. Unwilling to accept marginalized authors whose writing challenged the social construction of gendered social subjects, the literary establishment refused to grant legitimacy to the questions raised by these constructions. Undoubtedly, Barbachano Ponce was ahead of his time.

When reviewed, *El diario de José Toledo* received largely negative criticism. To this day, Federico Alvarez's article "José Toledo contra Barbachano Ponce," represents the most virulent attack on the novel. First, Alvarez objects to Barbachano Ponce's "erroneous and aliterary" use of the diary novel, admonishing him for not adhering to the rules defining the genre. His second point of contention, a question I will take up in the second part of this paper, has to do with José Toledo's fictional composition as a character. Alvarez condemns what he defines as José's "*feminoide*" characteristics, his "*cursilería*" which contributes, in his eyes, to the ridicule of (Mexican) homosexuality. I propose that this interpretation—such as those provided by most of Barbachano Ponce's detractors—derives from a misreading of *El diario de José Toledo.* I hope to demonstrate that such an interpretation, like those of most detractors of Barbachano Ponce's novel, derives from a reading conditioned by the ruling ideology on themes such as that of homosexuality or with respect to what constitutes a literary text.

Literary and Social Legitimacy: Supplement and Mimicry

I would first like to focus on the novel's literary quality, which Alvarez puts into question. Although the title of the novel suggests that it will read as a diary-novel, the reader does not find the common tropes nor the characteristics which traditionally constitute the genre.[6] Barbachano Ponce, as I intend to show, did not want to be bound by the rules of the genre. Rather, the word "diary" intimates the use of the genre as a literary device, fulfilling "the diary's potential as a literary strategy" (Abbott 18).

The novel is composed of two different kinds of narrations: the first-person narrative of José Toledo's diary, and a novellike-narration primarily in the third person which alternates with the diary entries. Each of José's entries is entitled *El diario de José Toledo* and marked by an undated day of the week. In the diary, the first-person "I" interplays with the second-person "you," and the past tense alternates with the present tense. The second-person narrative points to an addressee, Wenceslao, José's ex-lover. José relies on the present tense when referring to his letters to Wenceslao, but we find no epistolary exchange between the two characters, and José's letters are not transcribed in the diary. The messages in the letters are never revealed and the reader can only intimate from the entries in José's diary the content of those missives. However, this aspect of the novel invests the diary with qualities typical of the epistolary novel, therefore indicating the desire to engage in communication and to go beyond the notion of privacy and isolation specific to the diary. The second text, the novellike-narration in the third-person mentioned earlier, precisely performs the function of offsetting the lack of epistolary exchange, to add multivocality to the narration, and to develop themes that the diary only outlined. Moreover, I wish to argue that the third-person narration also serves to give the novel in its entirety a certain literary legitimacy, by producing a complex textual system. Let us pursue the notion of legitimacy.

At the end of the novel, the third-person narrator states that the diary was found in a bus. Abbott in his book on diary fiction, explains that "in the eighteenth century, the diary was employed to give the illusion of literary found object, something that people write but that is not supposed to be art" (18). I suggest that Barbachano Ponce chose to use the diary in half of his novel as a

---

[6]For an analysis of the genre and its conventions see Martens' *The Diary Novel*, Porter Abbott's *Diary Fiction*, and Field's *Form and Function in the Diary Novel*.

means to cross the boundaries between society and literature, between "high" and "low literature" (respectively, the novellike-narration and the 'literary' found object which is not supposed to be art), thus creating a device to bring to the fore such taboo issues as gender identity and homosexual desire. To give to José's narration the illusion of being "real," the author presents the idea that the diary was found. In the diary, the narration is centered exclusively around José's jealous and passionate love for Wenceslao, whereas the novellike-narration only alludes to homosexual love, resubmerging it into clandestinity, and displacing it with accounts of heterosexual relationships. In the novellike-narration "the closet still operates as a shaping presence" (Sedgwick, *Epistemology* 68) at the center of which stands Wenceslao and his denial of homosexuality. This type of veiled inscription of social and literary taboos acquiesces to the aesthetics of mainstream literature. It complies with the customary idea in most literary arenas that secrecy and clandestinity are the leaven of any good narration dealing with "difference." The second text is therefore encoded, and the reader faces long cryptic passages narrating Wenceslao's dreams. Yet the semantic field in these passages reasserts oppression, persecution, inertia, and anxiety:

> Wenceslao strolled along narrow side streets without exit, streets whose stone edges were grazed by green and tainted water. The mere thought of falling in it disgusted him. He wanted to flee from there. . . . Yet he found himself wandering again along narrow alleys. While trying to avoid the stinking puddle, he slipped falling into its slimy center. What once was a quagmire became an ocean of glaucous and stagnant water. (32)

The French literary magazine *Lire* devoted an issue in 1992 to homosexuality and writing. Once again, most of the authors agreed that to "avow the unavowable"—that is, in this case, homosexuality—during the act of writing, disempowers the literary text. The condition of writing, they add, is governed by secrecy, and the confession of homosexuality prevents the novel from becoming a "great book."[7] In the same vein, Alvarez denounces the diary's realism, which in his eyes detracts from the diary's "literary" quality: "A diary so real, so incredibly real, that it becomes unreadable, aliterary" (xvi). As if Barbachano Ponce anticipated this type of criticism he created the novellike-narration, the

---

[7]See Pierre Assouline's article "L'Homosexualité est-elle un atout littéraire?" and Roger Stéphane's interview "Entretien avec Roger Stéphane," in *Lire* 18-23.

"literary" component of the novel to be read not only as the "legitimate" text, but rather as a supplement, which Derrida defines in the following terms:

> The supplement adds itself, it is a surplus, a plenitude enriching another plenitude, the *fullest measure* of presence. It cumulates and accumulates presence. . . . Whether it adds or substitutes itself, the supplement is *exterior*, outside of the positivity to which it is super-added, alien to that which, in order to be replaced by it, must be other than it. Unlike the complement . . . the supplement is an exterior addition. (*Of Grammatology* 144–45)

In order for the diary to exist as a literary piece this exterior super-addition is vital. Alvarez considers what I chose to call the supplement as "the best part of the novel." This is the site of Barbachano Ponce's transgressive practice which escaped most critics. This text, the novellike-narration as supplement, diverted the attention of those readers who were not open to literary and social transgression, and it subversively confirmed the interdict, the "aliterary" text of the diary. The supplement possesses multiple powers of subversion, Derrida explains, because it

> has not only the power of procuring an absent presence through its image; procuring it for us through the proxy [procuration] of the sign, it holds it at a distance and masters it. For this presence is at the same time *desired* and *feared. The supplement transgresses and at the same time respects the interdict*" (Derrida, *Of Grammatology* 155; my emphasis).

The novellike-narration trangresses by positing itself as the literary plenitude enriching an "aliterary" plenitude, which is the diary. But at the same time it "respects the interdict" since the diary could not have its place within the artistic realm without the second text providing it with the "fullest measure of presence."

Furthermore, whereas critics commonly assume that a nonfiction text could not exist as a literary artefact without the type of supplementation we read in this novel, Barbachano Ponce was eager to show that texts, such as this diary, can effectively, and in an equally subversive fashion, supplement the literary one. Critics have too easily reduced the complexity of his composition by positing a mere manichean logic between two apparently incompatible texts. Nevertheless, the novellike-narration supplements the diary which in turn supplements its supplement. Barbachano Ponce could, in fact, be denouncing the exclusiveness of the taxonomic discourses which prevailed in the literary discourse of the time. With José's "coming out" in the diary (the aliterary text) Barbachano Ponce challenges "regimes of power/discourse," risking literary exclusion. Conversely, with such a character as Wenceslao, whose sexuality is socially and textually "closeted," he affirms and maintains social and literary decorum. Thus, by collapsing the aesthetic with the "real,"[8] Barbachano Ponce manages to debunk authoritative "texts," structured by sexual politics and literary conventions, while remaining within the framework of the literary conventions his novel seeks to undermine.[9] We might surmise that Barbachano Ponce subversively mimics the recognizable text within the production of literary discourse in order to give immanence to literary and social difference, to the diary and to homosexual desire. It is precisely through the analysis of the concept of mimicry in this novel that one can reveal the inextricability of the link between the diary and the novellike-narration, between their form and content.

In a recent study on gay and lesbian literature in Latin America, Foster devotes a few pages to *El diario de José Toledo.* He argues that the clichés of sentimental love in this novel could be read as "part of a bourgeois concept of heterosexual love that one variety of homosexual identity unfortunately, if not pathetically, *mimics*"(58; my emphasis). The notion of mimicry raised by Foster in the context of sexual identity formation in fiction is an important issue that needs to be examined more closely. Although Foster does not provide any specific examples, I would like to take up the question of what he might consider to be a pathetic mimicry of heterosexual behaviors.

José's narration mainly exposes the events which refer to Wenlescao, and the anguish caused by the breakup of their relationship. José's consuming

---

[8]The way José makes use of the diary reminds us of Gogol's novels, Gogol who, as Axthelm stated, "was among the first to recognize the fictional possibilities of the "ordinary" man, the petty official or clerk whose personal pains are compounded by an overwhelming sense of anonimity and humiliation" (7).

[9]At the same time, the concept of substitution, intrinsic to the Derridian definition of supplementarity, also leads us to read the second text as a product of sublimation (I use the definition of sublimation provided by Laplanche and Pontalis 431–33). This narration can be perceived as part of the artistic creation which Mexican society at that time held in "high esteem," while at the same time providing a space where the artist could sublimate what he and his readers most repressed: literary, social, and sexual marginality.

passion for Wenceslao permeates each line of the text and is rendered by an oppressive semantic composition. His emotional affliction shapes a text infused by pain and suffering. The constant repetition of such words as "desperate, anguish, suffer, ailing soul, cry, restless, agony. . . ," conveys José's continuous mortification, which in a sense constitutes the thematic foundation of the diary. The reiterative quality of the beginning of each entry also emphasizes the *quotidien* agonizing distress: "As usual, I got up early, waiting, as every morning, for your phone call. Monday, another sad day for me. . ." (13, 30, 13). This gives the narration a sense of circularity, with no exit, no future. However, this diary is not only based on self-observation or self-pity. Rather, it ventures to explain, to open itself up. First, this debunks the notion that a diary by definition is private. Still, José is less concerned with crossing the threshold between the private and the public than breaking away from the cultural practice of secrecy as exemplified in the novellike-narration. As Herdt puts it, secrecy, in the masonic sense of the term,[10] suggests complicity, maneuvering, and even conspiracy to overthrow hegemony. Yet when secrecy is not lived within a group or shared, we are in the realm of the "secret self." The notion of "secret self" implies separation from the social group which in turn allows for the hegemony to maintain "deviancies" imprisoned in the straightjacket of social conventions. In order to avoid the neurosis provoked by the hiding of the "self," José prefers to "confess." Although privacy is implied in the act of confessing,[11] it allows him

[10]I am indebted to Gilbert Herdt for his enticing analysis of the complex relationship between public, private, and secret which he recently presented at The Center for Twentieth Century Studies at Milwaukee in a paper entitled "Public, Private, and Secret: Secrecy and Individual Rights in Society" (1994).

[11]The semantically charged verb "to confess" requires on my part an explanation about how I use it. The fact that I link the notion of privacy with the act of confessing is undoubtedly due to my Catholic upbringing. What comes first to mind is the presence of a priest receiving a confession, a priest to whom one confides and who is bound by "professional secrecy." However, to use this verb in the context of this work has its dangers. In most dictionaries, to confess is "to tell or make known (as something wrong or damaging to oneself), to admit; to acknowledge sin to God, to disclose one's faults" (Webster's). The notion of wrongdoing and of sin, usually implied in the act of confessing, opens the door to a facile equation between José's confession and an admission of guilt. Yet when refering to José's confession I see a man expressing himself willfully about his acts, ideas, and feelings. He is not confessing blamable acts "murmuring low

to transcend his secret self. He defies the culturally prescribed notion of protection which in theory justifies the secret self. Rather than seeing protective qualities in the act of self-secrecy, José perceives it as a strategy to restrain and to control any "citizen" who may wish to open the secret self to the outside. Thus, by identifying his object of love as male, José reveals his homosexual desire, and his intention to go beyond the secret self. However, the act of confession endangers the self, which compels José to resort to problematic strategies such as the universalization of experiences, and consequently, mimicry.

The insistence, throughout the diary, on an impossible love and painful relationship, works to give his experience a sense of universality. It is made clear, throughout the narration, that society denounces homosexual love, alienating and stigmatizing those who engage in it, particularly if acting upon their desire.[12] José always refers to his love for Wenceslao in almost platonic terms, remaining chaste and controlled. This tendency to minimize the sexual encounter and to aestheticize sexuality accounts for José's hope for social inclusion through the universally shared experience of pain and love. These are concepts which transcend the notions of gender, class, and race. With this idea of commonality José wishes to neutralize indignation, and strives for acceptance. Several references in the text point to his concern to "cohere," yielding to the very society which placed him in a state of nonidentity: "I fell asleep kissing the bracelet and the medal my *husband* gave me the day we decided to unite for ever" (52; my emphasis).When referring to Wenceslao as his "husband," José clearly expresses what I choose to call a "coerced need" to remain within the institutionalized heterosexist gender, sexual, and economic framework. Clearly, José is at the threshold of the closet, not quite in, and not quite out either. At the same time, he invites the reader to cross the same boundaries, to enter the intimacy of the diary, to participate in the act of coming out. It is a cry for approval.

---

into priestly ears" (to use Gide's formulation). He is not admitting something he is ashamed of. He just wishes to come out. Yet I am aware of the fact that his coming out will always be construed as an evidence of guilt by those who already considered his "secret" as a sin.

[12]In the chapter on *Las púberes canéforas,* I note that in this novel homosexual intercourse does not define the characters' sexual identity if the person engages in sexual activity in exchange for monetary or other types of material gain. In *El diario de José Toledo,* this is equally true. Wenceslao's parents are aware of their son's relationship with José. Although they opposed it, they tolerate it because of the financial help José gives to Wenceslao.

Catholicism and faith is another cultural paradigm on which José draws in order to "undercut"—as Johnson puts in her article on Hurston—"the absoluteness of the opposition" between gay and straight people (322). Throughout his narration, José confides in God, and especially in the Virgin Mary—the mother of all Mexicans[13]—praying for assistance, and emphasizing that all Christians are worthy of mercy and forgiveness. Later however, José feels abandoned and enters a phase of guilt and self-recrimination, characteristic of Christian morality:

> The Virgin Mary does not listen to me any longer, nor does she help me; I think she has forgotten me for ever. . . . I plead God and the Virgen for your return. . . . I plead although my love for you has damned me. But I cannot remedy it, and perhaps, when death comes, I will have to pay for I am guilty of a love that does not correspond to the love of a normal person. (43–86)

Moreover, as mentioned earlier, José's narration transcends introspection by addressing itself to Wenceslao. But the protagonist also alludes to a multiplicity of characters who are part of his daily life: his colleagues from work, his family, his friends. The second narration provides a space for the literary and social development of these characters. Each section of text following a diary entry, has a title with the names of Wenceslao and the characters present in the particular segment. Interestingly enough, all the "straight" characters are also wracked by despair because of personal problems. Socorro, José's sister, is expecting a child outside of marriage, and she has to confront her father's anger and society's reprobation; Carrin's wife is having an affair; both Wenceslao's and José's mothers think that they have failed in their marriages and as individuals.

One could indeed, as Foster suggests, read José's behavior, and diagnose it as fitting the economy of "compulsory heterosexuality," to use Rich's term coined in her work on lesbian sexuality and its representations. However, it is important to emphasize that during the late 1950s, social and literary inscription

---

[13]Mexican painter Nahum B. Zenil is also an artist who turns to the misericordious image/figure of the Virgen of Guadalupe. In his *retablo* Bendiciones (Blessings, 1990), he represents two men whose relationship, according to art critic Edward Sullivan, "society disapproves of. In their quest for freedom they are protected by the Virgen of Guadalupe-deity, sustaining mother and earth goddess" (72).

of homosexuality in Mexico was already a subversive challenge to these institutions. To inscribe homosexuality as a site of difference aiming at different representations of love and pain, was most probably viewed by certain authors as too radical. Furthermore, Herdt also reminds us in his work on secrecy, that they still had to create a language to express feelings and attitudes that were unclassifiable. This could be said of Barbachano Ponce's novel. Yet couldn't Barbachano Ponce have resorted to the notion of commonality, as such critics as Johnson suggested in another context, to "disguise, to dissimilate, to resemble rather than contrast," as the idea of "sameness allows for the social and literary inscription of unsameness?" Shouldn't we then reconsider the notion of mimicry?

The field of psychoanalysis and of colonial studies provides us with interesting and innovative ways to conceive the concept of mimicry when dealing with the colonial subject, and by extension, with the problem of identity formation of sexual, cultural, and social minorities. Bhabha's clarification of Lacan's definition of mimicry is particularly relevant to this study. Bhabha writes that "mimicry is like camouflage, not a harmonization or reppression of difference but a form of resemblance that differs/defends presence by displacing it in part, metonymically" (131).[14] Doesn't José's diary, and his expression of love and pain, constitute a way of defending its literary and social presence?

Bhabha goes on to say that "mimicry is the desire for a reformed, *recognizable other*, as a subject of a difference that is *almost the same, but not quite*. . . . [Yet] the menace of mimicry is its *double* vision which in disclosing the ambivalence [of heterosexual discourse, in the case of our study] also disrupts its authority" (126–29; emphasis in original). This elucidation of mimicry allows us to recontextualize and to reassess Barbachano Ponce's work keeping in mind the challenging question of mimeticism and representation.

Mimicry might be construed as representing immanence, negative difference, or normativeness. But it should also be rethought as Bhabha does it, in terms of a device, a strategy which allows to subvert, to disturb from within textually and socially based representations, and to undermine sexual difference.

---

[14]Bhabha's article is foreworded by an epigraph gleaned from Lacan's *Four Fundamental Concepts of Psycho-Analysis:* "Mimicry reveals something in so far as it is distinct from what might be called an itself that is behind. The effect of mimicry is camouflage. . . . It is not a question of harmonizing with the background, but against a mottled background, of becoming mottled—exactly like the technique of camouflage practiced in human warfare"(99).

José Toledo or The Emasculation of the Mexican Gay Male

Barbachano Ponce's inscription of homosexuality opens another complex line of issues. The most polemical one springs from Alvarez's critique which views José's sensibility as a "trope of the female soul in a man's body" (Silverman 339). Before I begin to examine the social implications of this type of critique, I would like to provide essential cultural and historical markers in order for us to understand why the image of strong masculinity within homosexuality has been mainstreamed in Mexican literary narrativization and in its fictional construction of gay characters.

As Monsiváis argues in a recent article on the consequences of the "sexual revolution" in Mexico, the feminist movements of the 1970s opened the road for dramatic changes in sexual behaviors (174). This lead to an increasing participation of women in the social, economic, and political realms as well as in the legal field which revindicated equality with men. Monsiváis also attributes those changes to the process of secularization, or as he puts it, the "*descatolización*" (de-Catholicization) of México (169). In the late 1950s and the early 1960s, sexism and moral judgement strongly prevailed. Although, since 1917, the church continually lost political power, the effect of Catholicism on sexuality, and particularly on gay sexuality, still defined, to a great extent, sexual identity formations.

In his review of Cantarella's book on bisexuality in the ancient world, Griffin reminds us that "when Christianity came into power [in Rome], Saint Paul inherited from the Old Testament a complete condemnation of homosexual acts, (especially in strong contrast with Greek ideas) of the active partner, who caused defilement and who sowed on stony ground the seed which should have engendered children for the people of Israel" (30). Further, Griffin explains that by the end of the fourth century "passive homosexuals, rather than active ones, took the brunt of the anger of Christian emperors, because the church wanted to condemn all homosexuals, but compromised in the face of the opposition of traditional pagan society by punishing only the perennial unpopular group [the passive homosexual]" (30).

In Mexico, as in many other countries dominated by centuries of practicing Catholicism, the hegemony of male order and "phallic masculinity," as exemplified by the patriarchal family, remained unchallenged. In her book *Plotting Women*, Franco includes a revealing passage by Ignacio Ramírez who, in 1886, wrote that "all nations owe their fall and ignominity to a woman"(xviii). Indeed

Ramírez could have provided many accounts of this type of historicization of woman. The Christian myth around Eve who denied humanity the right to a world without pain and suffering is only one of them. In Mexico, Doña Marina or the Malinche is *the* historical person to "fit the bill of the female treachery" as Franco puts it (xviii). Franco adds that Paz in his *El laberinto de la soledad* (*Labyrinth of Solitude*; 1950)

> located the 'Mexican disease' precisely in this ambiguous subjectivity of the sons of the Malinche who were shamed by her rape (conquest) and thus forced to reject the feminine in themselves as the devalued, the passive, the mauled and battered, as la chingada, the violated, the one that has been screwed over, fucked, and yet is herself the betrayer. (xix)

Samuel Ramos went even further in his book *El perfil del hombre y de la cultura en México* (*A Profile of Man and Mexican Culture*; 1934), where he posited that:

> The phallic obsession of the *pelado* does not bear comparison with phallic cults, which are based on the idea of fecundity and eternal life. The phallus suggests to the *pelado* the idea of power. This gave rise to a very impoverished definition of manhood. Since the *pelado* is a shallow human being, he strives to fill his void with the only valour within his reach: the bravery of the macho. This popular definition of men has become a fatal prejudice for every Mexican. When compared with the foreign and civilized man which reveals his "nonexistence" or insignificancy, the Mexican consoles himself in the following way: 'a European—he says— has science, art, technology, and so on; we have nothing of that sort here, but . . . we are real men. (Monsiváis, *Escenas de pudor* 105)

Therefore in order to *be* Mexican you had *to be a man*; "*tener muchos güevos* was the only language for magnificence" adds Monsiváis (104; having balls is the only language for greatness). "To be a man" was considered to be the highest social honor, the epitome of successful social conduct, of social order. Signs of femininity ("fragility, sensibility, refinement") would irremediably void masculinity, for the "macho" can only be so by reaffirming women's inferiority. *To be a man* even became the essence of Mexicaness, thereby implicitly denying women the right to Mexican national identity.

It is important to remember that homophobia's roots are not to be found only in Catholicism. Lumsden points out, for example:

> Aztec rulers executed anyone practicing sodomy within their territories in the central altiplano. Especially severe punishments were reserved for the "cuiloni" or passive and effeminate sex partners, who were burned to death after their entrails were ripped out via the orifice which customarily served them as sex organ. Moreover, unlike many other indigenous groups in North America, in which "berdaches" were common and respected by the indigenous cultures, the Aztecs executed any man caught dressed as a woman. (14)[15]

Lumsden adds that in many cases the Spanish exaggerated homosexuality among indigenous populations in the Americas "because the custom of 'nefarious sin' among natives could be used to justify their 'civilizing mission' in the New Spain" (14).

This "history" might explain the logic behind Alvarez's thinking. Alvarez, who, although responsive to the systematic closeting of gay issues in literature, could write the following about José's representation: "Choosing a ridiculous homosexual, banal, lacking sensibility, spiritual richness, imagination, ingenuity (not to mention talent) . . . is to imply that all homosexuals are the same . . . . [All these characteristics] little by little shape his *'feminoide' psychology*" (2–3; my emphasis). The word "cursi" does not go unnoticed here. In her study of the concept of the "cursi," Noël Valis explains that within the Spanish context of the nineteenth century, the "cursi" was frequently an equivalent of the feminine. According to Valis, "the *cursi* was a trap of unstable appearances, in which front and back, inside and outside, visible and invisible, told different stories, but came to the same conclusion/accusation: *cursilona*!" (5). If as Valis adds, "the cursi" is paradigmatic of the marginalization of those who wish to be what they are not supposed to be; "the cursi results from undesirable social displacements

---

[15]Among the references used by Lumsden, those of Salvador Novo, *Las locas, el sexo, los burdeles* (1972); Noemí Quezada, *Amor y magia entre los aztecas* (1989); María Isabel Morgan, "La sexualidad en la sociedad azteca" in *Familia y sexualidad. La educación de la sexualidad humana*, vol. 1 (1979); Julia Tuñón Pablos, *Mujeres en México: una historia olvidada* (1987); David Thorstad, "A Pueblo Journal: Homosexuality Among the Zapotecs," *Christopher Street* 160 (March 1988), are noteworthy.

. . . it lacks depth, lacks substance. Aesthetically, it offends" (6–10), then it is no surprise that Alvarez should resort to a word so semantically loaded as "cursilería" to express his disapproval.[16]

Yet this perception—a feminine, therefore tarnished, image of homosexuality—is rather unsettling if one examines what it implies about the social construction of homosexuality. Again, there is no doubt that heterosexual males—even females—could contain José in the cultural stereotype which tends to negatively associate femininity with homosexuality. Nevertheless, we could also present this novel as an effort to denounce "rugged machismo," and to engage in a reconceptualization of the "semantically overcharged" notion of virility in Mexico.[17] After all, Paz himself wrote that the sentence "'I am your father' does not have a paternal flavor, nor is it uttered to protect, to shield or drive; rather, it wishes to impose a superiority in order to humiliate" (73). As I mention in the previous chapter, in countries like Mexico, males tended to consider sexuality between men as an extension of male bonding. Homosexuality should not in anyway undermine manliness (*hombría*), and as long as it is not associated with passivity, inertia, and overture, but rather with activity, aggressiveness, and closure, homosexuality cannot be dismissed, much less ridiculed.

---

[16]I want to transcribe here the manifesto of a group of Mexican intellectuals written in 1934, which appears in *Escenas de pudor y liviandad* by Monsiváis: "Given the attempt to purify the public administration, we request that such efforts be extended to individuals of doubtful morality holding public office and those who by their effeminate actions, not only constitute an example worthy of punishment, but also create an atmosphere of corruption that reaches such a point that it prevents the rooting of manly virtues in our youth. . . . If we were to combat the presence of fanatics and reactionaries in public office, we must also combat the presence of the hermaphrodite, who is incapable of identifying with workers in the current reform" (110). Among the signatories: José Rubén Romero, Mauricio Magdaleno, Rafael Muñoz, Mariano Silvo y Aceves, Renato Leduc, Juan O'Gorman, Xavier Icaza, Francisco L. Urquizo, Emilio Abreu Gómez, Humberto Tejera, Héctor Pérez Martínez, and Julio Jímenez Rueda.

[17]As I mention elsewhere, as early as the 1950s, many of Barbachano Ponce's plays and their themes questioned the social configuration of gender relation, the hegemony of heterosexual epistemology. He was also a precursor of bringing together two tropes of difference, race and homosexuality, in contemporary Mexican letters.

It is not so much the idea of same-sex desire that Mexican culture questions. It is the idea that men could actually degrade themselves by acknowledging femininity within their homosexuality, forcing them to cross the boundaries between genders, and "collapse gender divisions." Alvarez's critique of José's "deviant masculinity" suggests that Barbachano Ponce might have written a homophobic novel, since he could not transcend the cultural stereotype based on this trope of inversion ("woman's soul enclosed in a man's body"), a true reflection of traditional homophobic Mexican attitudes. For Alvarez, José's femininity takes away from himself, and by extension from the homosexual community at large, the most legitimate part of themselves, their masculinity. By doing so, the feminine prohibits any acting out of masculine roles, the essence of manliness/Mexicaness.

It seems to me that Barbachano Ponce's representation of José could be read differently. We could see this composition as a way to debunk another deeply entrenched cultural stereoptype in Mexico: the one which insidiously posits as a norm that male same-sex desire can only be conceived within the parameters of masculinity, and which impedes, if not violently condemns, homosexuals who acknoweledge and wish to act out their femininity. According to this perspective, we understand this novel as a process of unlearning assumptions, as a "subversive alignment" with femininity. It also presents a way to eschew conventional masculinity by offering other paradigms of sexual identity. Furthermore, Silverman cogently suggests that "we must entertain the possibility that a gay man might deploy signifiers of femininity not only because to do so is to generate a counterdiscourse, but because an identification with "woman" constitutes the very basis of his identity, and/or the position from which he desires" (Silverman, *Male Subjectivity* 344). While Barbachano Ponce's inscription of homosexual desire could be construed as a sign of homophobia, Alvarez's critique can in turn be interpreted as emerging from a profound misogynistic position.

In spite of the book's apparent straightforwardness, and the seemingly facile reaffirmation of a prejudicial cultural stereotype, Barbachano Ponce questions the traditional stability of these norms pointing to the "unreconciled ambivalence" in Mexican culture between femininity and masculinity, heterosexuality and homosexuality. This novel, and the diary sections in particular, function as the *thetic* which Kristeva defines as

> that crucial space on the basis of which the human being constitutes himself as signifying and/or social. . . . It is the very place textual experience aims toward. In this sense, textual experience represents one of

> the most daring explorations the subject can allow himself, one that delves into the constitutive process. But at the same time and as a result, textual experience reaches the very foundation of the social . . . that which is exploited by sociality but which elaborates and can go beyond it, while distorting and transforming it." (*Texto de la novela* 67)

José loses his diary on the 27th of October, 1958. One month later at the age of twenty, on November the 20th, he commits suicide by jumping out a window. Many things could explain such an act: the loss of the diary which provided him emotional release, the possibility that everybody might actually learn the contents of the diary; the hopelessness of ever being able to share his love with Wenceslao; and ultimately the social negation of the position from which he desires. The act of suicide clearly speaks of José's desperation. However, death does not only chastize José's act of transgression. We know that his death predates the second narration, the one the author acknowledges as "his." The publication of the book as two supplements supplementing each other, and the challenging inscription of homosexuality as "nonphallic masculinity," made Barbachano Ponce, in the eyes of the literary community and of society, doubly complicitous with José. This induces another kind of suicide, the professional suicide of Barbachano Ponce who, after publishing his novel as "edición del autor," had to withdraw, and was excluded from the literary scene for more than twenty years. This certainly delayed the coming out of gay and lesbian characters as well as their "coming in" the history of Mexican literature.

CHAPTER 6: *AMORA* OR IGNORANCE VIS-À-VIS MAIEUTICS AND DIALECTICS

The words of the introductory text which Rosamaría Roffiel chooses as a prologue to her novel shed significant light on its composition:

> Yes, in fact, this is a very *autobiographical* novel. Almost all the characters really exist. Almost all the *names were changed* and almost everything *really happened*. I dedicate it to my women friends . . . who enriched these pages with their commentaries, their experiences, their sense of humor and above all with their unassailable friendship. . . . I also dedicate it to all the women who dare to love women. (2; emphasis mine)

Although this prologue emphasizes the qualifying term "autobiographical," it invites the reader from the start to relate author and text to a degree beyond a mere authorial link. The type of autobiography Roffiel offers, for instance, breaks with the contractual dimension that Lejeune assigns to autobiography and which posits that the name on the title page, the signature, defines autobiographical identity. To begin with, *Amora* is presented as a novel, and autobiography is not taken here as another "genre or a mode, but [as] a figure of reading or of understanding that occurs, to some degree, in all texts. The autobiographical moment happens as an alignment between the two subjects involved in the process of reading in which they determine each other by mutual reflexive substitution" (De Man 70). The novel does not begin with a personal experience nor in the narrator's voice. In addition, though the text undoubtedly is organized around the narrator's "self," the latter is surrounded at the same time by a multiplicity of voices without which the "self" and "self-knowledge" would have no place. As De Man cogently argues,

> The spectacular moment that is part of all understanding reveals the tropological structure that underlies all cognitions, including the knowledge of self. The interest of autobiography, then, is not that it reveals reliable self-knowledge—it does not—but that it demonstrates in a striking way the impossibility of closure and totalization (that is the

> impossibility of coming into being) of all textual systems made up of tropological substitutions. (71)

The kind of autobiography Amora proposes clearly wishes to "overcome specularity," to escape from the totalizing notion of authenticity and from what De Man calls "the coercions of the tropological system" (71–72).

The choice of the narrator's name Guadalupe and not Rosamaría, is an ingenious way of circumventing "the tropological system of the name." The almost generic quality of a name as semantically loaded as Guadalupe allows the author to emphasize the experiential side of her biography, while at the same time aspiring, if not to share the experience, at least to refer to it as an experience common to the majority of Mexican women, an experience with which they are able to identify. In fact, Guadalupe could be any Mexican woman or man. As Jacques Lafaye reminds us in his seminal studies on the Virgin of Guadalupe, the name Guadalupe is widespread especially in its abbreviated form Lupe and is given indiscriminately to both man and woman (16). This fact allows the identification to go beyond the feminine realm and gives the largest possible number of Mexicans access to the debate proposed by *Amora*. As the prologue states, the novel is directed principally to women, though it also includes those who struggle to widen the discourse around sexuality and its politicization. Taking into account the devotion of Mexicans to the Virgin of Guadalupe and the place she occupies in their hearts, the choice of the name Guadalupe is a wise one. How could one forget that the name Guadalupe coincides with the mere mention of truly important events of Mexican history? Nearly all these events were the result of popular uprisings against injustices striking a large number of Mexican citizens. The first Mexican separatists in 1880 adopted the name of "the Guadalupes." Father Hidalgo, Morelos, Zapata, and Villa, among the most notable, gathered their partisans in different moments of history around the banner of Our Lady of Guadalupe (Lafaye 16). Giving the narrator the name Guadalupe invites readers to join the cause against the intolerance surrounding social difference. In the context of the history narrated by this "autobiographical" novel, that is, the history of women who dare to love other women, the act of choosing a name which does not necessarily reflect the gender of its bearer contributes moreover to destabilizing the morphological authoritativeness which the name traditionally confers. If, as Judith Butler explains, the name constitutes "a site of identification, a site where the dynamic of identification is at play," then the name Guadalupe here becomes "the site of a certain crossing, a transfer of gender" (*Bodies That Matter* 143–44). In this novel the name does not promise the stability of what is named, nor does it guarantee the permanence of meaning. The name Guadalupe implies a plural identity.

The autobiographical text is here a product of hybridity since it feeds itself to a great extent on the plurality and multiplicity that make up the intimate individual experience. Lejeune warns that "telling the truth about oneself, constituting oneself as a complete subject, is an imaginary act" (427). Thus it is understood that the important thing in this autobiography is not so much "telling the truth about oneself," but rather the shading of individual experience through the collective. This impels Roffiel to adopt a transparent written language, "a referential transparency" which allows her to fully express herself, while at the same time offering to the other male/female Guadalupes an opportunity to collaborate in this process of expression. On the one hand, the aesthetic exploration is obvious, as is witnessed by what can be called the lyrical chapters which make up this novel. On the other, the readers are informed from the prologue that "everything really happened." This statement, however, does not imply that what "really happened" will give rise to a "truthful discourse." One need only recall the definitions of the concepts of "reality" and "truth." Reality is defined as something real, something constituted not only as a concept but as a thing. It consists of that which effectively exists, as opposed to the imagination or the representation of that which exists. Truth is defined as the "conformity of things with the concept which the mind forms of them. It implies conformity of what is spoken with what is felt or thought." Hence truth requires the consent of the spirit, "an internal coherence of thought" (*Diccionario de la Real Academia*). This novel is presented as real by virtue of the fact that Roffiel is "struggling to inscribe experience on historically available forms of representation" (De Lauretis's formula, "Sexual" 161). *Amora* does not pretend to be truthful, however, since, as will be seen later, the very structure of the novel untiringly questions the concept of truth.

The way in which Roffiel's work is composed and organized makes reference to the classical Greek period. First, the type of autobiography we are reading here could very well find its origin in the ancient autobiographical form, above all in the essentially public nature of the autobiography. In his chapter on "Forms of Time and of the Chronotopes in the Novel," Mikhail Bakhtin observes that "in ancient times the autobiographical and biographical self-consciousness of an individual and his life was first laid bare and shaped in the public square" (*Dialogic* 131). It seems that in *Amora* the individual consciousness which the narrator has of herself is inseparable from the context that surrounds her. Her private self is similar to that which she presents the public, the "utter exteriority of the individual" for whom "to be exterior meant to be for others, for the collective, for one's own people" (*Dialogic* 135). She aspires to a public self (as a subject, as a lesbian) which can be expressed as was customary in ancient times, in the agora where all participate.[1] For the Greek of the classical period, Bakhtin reminds us, "every aspect of existence could be seen and heard. . . . A mute internal life, a mute grief, mute thought, were completely foreign to the Greek. All this—that is, his entire internal life— could exist only if manifested externally in audible or visible form" (*Dialogic* 134).

The analogy established here, between this *fin de siècle* novel and certain modes of expression of ancient Greece, may seem at first unwarranted. After all, we live in an era of globalization and in a world of communication in which, as the French philosopher Michel Serres comments, we are all messengers (see *Hermes*). *Amora* considers anew the very concept of communication. The fact that we are all messengers and that we all receive messages does not erase, however, the fact that we are living in a century that is "very dry, very intellectual, judicial and scientific" (Serres 93), in which we do not hear ourselves, lost in the confusion which the plethora of messages brings. *Amora* invites us not only to participate in the circulation of ideas, but also to a true contact, a reciprocity, a relational transmission. Its intent is to save its characters and itself from muteness, from invisibility, from the loneliness in which, paradoxically, the globalization of communication keeps them, in order to find anew "the popular chronotope of the public square" that appears to have been lost (*Dialogic* 135). There is no room in this novel for silence.[2] The social silence imposed upon the marginalized is replaced by an explosion of words, burst secrets, and externalizations of emotions. There is no absence or feeling of guilt. Silence must be and is confronted.

The structure of *Amora* also recalls the dialogues of Socrates transcribed by Plato as conversations remembered and framed within a story. "At the root

---

[1]It should not be ignored, however, that in ancient times the individual underwent examination by his fellow-citizens, who judged him and his actions, in the public square. In *Amora* the public square is transformed (or is it defined utopically?) instead into a place of tolerance and coexistence, a place for all. It would not be a place at the margin of official society as were the squares in European cities of the thirteenth and fourteenth centuries, but rather the place where civil society is constituted (see *Dialogic* 132).

[2]Debra Castillo in her chapter "On silence," shows convincingly that the female narrators in novels written by women tend to appropriate the silence which patriarchal society imposes on them in order to subvert it, even when they keep it as a principal "protagonist" in the narration.

of the genre," Bakhtin explains,

> . . . is found the Socratic notion of the dialogic nature of truth, and the dialogic nature of human thought about truth. The dialogical methods for seeking truth are placed against the official monologism which attempts to hold/possess a ready-made truth, and moreover they are placed against the naive self-confidence of those who think they know something, that is, those who believe they are in possession of certain truths. (*Problems* 110)

In effect, the novel as a whole is built around a series of dialogues between the narrator and several of her female friends, lovers, professional colleagues, and members of her family. The main object of these dialogues is the discussion of the concept of sexual gender, sexuality, and the determining factors in sexual relationships. In her influential article "Sexual Indifference," De Lauretis, turning to Halperin's reading of Plato's Symposium, remind us that Plato hoped to "prescribe erotic reciprocity between human beings, a reciprocity whose philosophical signification was translated fundamentally in the form of dialogue" (157). De Lauretis points out a central problem in the way in which erotic reciprocity is defined in several of the dialogues of Plato. In these dialogues, Halperin explains, the concept of sexual pleasure is fused, with respect to women, to the reproductive or generative function: "It is indeed so grounded in the text, both rhetorically (Diotima's language systematically conflates sexual pleasure with the reproductive or generative function), and narratively, in the presumed experience of a female character, since to the Greeks female sexuality differed from male sex precisely in that sexual pleasure for women was intimately bound up with procreation" (157). De Lauretis demonstrates how this fusion leads Halperin deeper into the Platonic doctrine and its sexual gender politics. In his critical analysis Halperin concludes that in Plato "the interdependence of sexual reproductive abilities is in reality a physiological characteristic of the man and not the woman." Halperin adds that this doctrine, as a consequence, advocates appropriation of the feminine by the masculine, "a feminine built from masculine paradigms" (157). De Lauretis carries this conclusion even farther by demonstrating that "the appropriation of the feminine for the erotic ethos of a social intellectual elite . . . had the effect not only of securing the millenary exclusion of women from philosophical dialogue, and the absolute excision of nonreproductive sexuality from the Western discourse on love" (158). Roffiel, by resorting to the Socratic dialogical method, is not thereby embracing the Platonic ideology questioned by Halperin and De Lauretis. Following the initial precepts of Socratic dialogue, Roffiel instead moves toward an opening, affirming the need for reinserting women into philosophical dialogue. *Amora*'s narrator states that she is not sure of anything, and through the dialogue she intends everyone to recognize that they don't know either, that there can be no ready-made answers. At the same time admitting her ignorance, she takes up the task of spurring her interlocutors to debunk dogmatic certainties. She follows the Socratic philosophy in which the desire to live better implies a constant search, far removed from definitive knowledge. She makes use of the two most notable strategies of the Socratic dialogues which will be studied throughout this analysis: syncrisis and anacrisis. Syncrisis is understood "as the juxtaposition of various points of view upon a specific object" and anacrisis "as a means of provoking words from the interlocutor forcing him to express his opinion thoroughly" (*Problems* 111). Anacrisis consists of going beyond preconceived ideas, "clarifying them with the word and in that way exposing the falsity and incomplete state of these ideas. . . . Anacrisis is the provocation of the word with the word" (*Problems* 111). Irony is another of the strategies privileged in *Amora*. Guadalupe pretends not to know in order to make her interlocutor comprehend what is "certain," that is, to realize that she knows nothing and only thinks she knows.

There are no idle conversations in this novel. The narrator surrenders herself to an interrogative dialogue, a dialogue which might initiate an opening and an awakening of consciousness in a repressive Mexico, leading the thinking word into circulation as reflection. However, even though Guadalupe initiates the interrogative dialogue, she allows her interlocutors to subject her to the same kind of questioning. This critical process is disturbing, as it strips the person questioned of his/her certitudes, taking away the presumptuousness of the person who thinks s/he knows, at the same time highlighting the conformism that surrounds rash certainties. The narrator favors interaction between languages and ideologies. What is most fascinating in this novel is that the word is considered a privileged component in human relationships. The power of the word frees the person who subjects it to a critical examination. In this novel the dialectical exercise consists of transforming speech into a custom for harmonizing human relationships and making the world an intelligible place through the agency of the word. Guadalupe is not presented as a female philosopher interpellating the world, but rather as someone who aspires to transform the world. As we will see below, however, the Socratic method is not infallible.

In the introduction to her book on autobiography in Latin America, Silvia Molloy excludes from the autobiographical genre those works whose "central concern is not autobiographical," works in which "the narration of the self is more a means to achieve an end than the end itself" (3). As mentioned earlier, in *Amora* the self is not the exclusive subject of the novel, and in the process of construction and deconstruction of this self, it is expected that other selves will be moved to "self-confrontation." But if, as Molloy points out, this type of writing is only autobiographical "tangentially," how do we explain the need to define *Amora* as autobiographical in the prologue? Molloy herself observes that "self-reflective writing is a form of exposure that begs for understanding" (6). The notion of exposure and unmasking is central here. The process of identification for Roffiel is initiated from the beginning of the novel, without any room for confusion. Guadalupe is a feminist and lesbian, and Roffiel identifies herself in the same way: we are not witnessing a displacement of identities nor a self-covering on the part of Roffiel, rather, she assumes a certain authority. This is a way of creating solidarity with the other voices in the text attempting to understand themselves and open themselves with the hope that intolerance will not deny them their "selves." In this context the autobiographical reference "functions as an act of communication" (Lejeune 422) in which "the mediating text that governs the self-portrait" of Guadalupe (Molloy 67) would be the dialogue, or better yet the dialoguing voices.[3]

What motivates these dialectical debates in *Amora*? What stimulates the argumentative dialogue in this text?

The Dialogists and the Object of the Argumentative Dialogue

The story framing the dialogues is the narration of an amorous relationship between Guadalupe, the self-taught feminist lesbian journalist, and Claudia, daughter of a wealthy bourgeois family, a heterosexual ten years younger than

---

[3]In addition to the works on autobiography mentioned so far, I would like to point out the following complementary studies: James Olney, ed., *Metaphors of Self: The Meaning of Autobiography* (Princeton, 1972) and *Autobiography: Essays Theoretical and Critical* (Princeton, 1980); Elizabeth Bruss, *Auto-Acts: The Changing Situation of a Literary Genre* (Johns Hopkins, 1976); William Spengeman, *The Forms of Autobiography* (Yale, 1980); Estelle Jelinek, ed., *Women's Autobiography: Essays and Criticism* (Indiana, 1980); Guy Mercadier, ed., *L'Autobiographie dans le monde hispanique* (Aix-en-Provence, 1980); Roy Pascal, *Design and Truth in Autobiography* (Garland, 1985); Sidonie Smith, *A Poetics of Women's Autobiography: Marginality and the Fiction of Self-Representation* (Indiana, 1987); Shari Benstock, ed., *The Private Self: Theory and Practice of Women's Autobiographical Writing* (Chapel Hill, 1988).

Guadalupe. The fact that everything separates these two women socially will give rise to a series of reflections, questions, and polemics, through which they attempt to examine the role of feminist movements in Mexico, their successes and failures, and their relationship with lesbianism. The most interesting thing, however, is that Amora extends the debate over feminism by posing problems that emerge when one limits oneself to a single, unified definition of the term feminism: "I suppose there are as many feminisms as there are women in the world" (75). Above all this novel exposes the dissensions arising between women in the act of defining feminist consciousness.

The group of "dialogists" is made up of several women whose lives Guadalupe shares directly or indirectly. Lupe works closely with Victoria, a sociologist in the Rape Victims' Support Group. Norma lives in a neighboring apartment and is a friend of Lupe; she is the most radical lesbian feminist of the group. Graciela and Gloria also live in the same building, but they represent more traditional Mexican women: Gloria has still not recovered from her divorce, having lost custody of her only child whom she has not seen since. Graciela has a relationship with Alberto, who cheats on her with other women and then returns to Graciela's apartment as if it were a boarding house, to eat and have his clothes washed. Graciela and Gloria have little education or experience in the struggle for women's liberation. They are located at the other end of the spectrum; as they embody traditionalism, their voices contribute to maintaining a certain balance in the conversations, which tend, as will be seen, to delve into essentialist discourses on the question of sexual difference.

Mariana and Citlali are Lupe's two roommates. Though feminists and lesbians, Mariana, Citlali, and Guadalupe do not make up a uniform group. It is worth noting that Guadalupe refers to the others as her "family." This urgency to form a family is remarkable. The idea of possessing a space of one's own is one that few would contest at this point. However, the family, as Lupe understands it ("the three of us have formed a family and made a temple of our space" (24)), goes against the restricted sense assigned to this institution in Mexican and other societies. No ties of kinship bind the three women; they are not joined by marriage, nor by filiation. The three women, therefore, are attempting to redefine the concept of family, while also seeking to assure a genealogy, a "descent," like any other family with blood ties. This type of nucleus will give birth to new generations of women who will find the support, the determination, and the inspiration needed to establish in turn their own "families." The space of the home for Lupe no longer represents a place of confinement or restriction, but rather a place of re-creation, a dialectical space between the intimate and the exterior, a place precisely destabilizing the traditional boundary between the public and the private. Furthermore, the rare moments of introspection refer constantly to this new type of nuclear family whose ties must be reinforced. Lupe finds a parallel between the evolution of her own life and that of the women's liberation movement in Mexico. With almost documentary precision she invites the reader to join the movement and she emphasizes the inseparability of the constitution of her individuality in this historical and social context. Lupe's self is born together with this liberation movement which guides her to the discovery of her subjectivity, a subjectivity that seeks perpetually to redefine itself. The process of self-redefinition is only possible if one begins likewise a reevaluation of feminism in Mexico. Several recurrent concerns stand out in this novel: that of consciousness-raising and finding solutions in order to relieve the extemporaneous nature of the social-judicial system, and that of challenging and reforming the language which keeps women in a marginalized cultural position.[4]

She describes specific cases of injustice in which the police, the Public Ministry, and the courts are accomplices. She devotes several pages to the "crime of rape":

> But if you know the guy's name, the place where he works, where he lives, why can't you throw him in jail? Because in this country, the crime of rape is the only one where the victim has to prove she is a victim. . . . They all pay ridiculous bails, or bribes, and get off as free as the wind. In the Support Group we had a case where the sentence was to pay the victim two thousand pesos because her blouse ripped during the attack, and the judge—get this, a woman judge!—decided that was the price of the piece of clothing and the payment was enough. (29–30)

In particular she points to the fact that the male gender still makes the laws; the presence of women judges, therefore, is not sufficient to change the patriarchal system *in situ*. Following French and North American feminist theo-

---

[4]From the first pages the influence of theories proposed by French feminism in the last twenty years can be felt, in particular those of the critic-philosophers Luce Irigaray and Hélène Cixous, who are among the first feminists to denounce and deconstruct symbolic systems such as art, religion, the family and above all, language which excludes woman as a subject. In the same way, one finds anew in *Amora* the combination of various genres in a single text, such as autobiography, essay, poetic prose, reminiscent of French feminist criticism.

ries, one would say that there are situations in *Amora* in which the narrator discredits the very language which for centuries have subjected women to degrading "metaphors":

> What can I get for you, *madrecitas*?
> First off, we are not your mothers. . . .
> Where does he get off with *madrecitas*? Never in all my fucking life would it occur to me to have a son as ugly as him. . . . What happens is that they're accustomed to women letting them say anything. (56)

She emphasizes her dissatisfaction with language through various paradigms, and she reflects in ever greater detail on the act of naming with respect to women who manifest their sexual preferences (76–78, 111, 82–83).

These reevaluations are constructed in the context of the problems that the relationship between Claudia and Lupe poses for each of the women. Claudia is the most important character. In fact her relationship with Lupe constitutes the central thematic axis of the novel. Lupe and Claudia's status as a couple allows for the introduction, from the very first chapter, of the theme of female homosexuality, and instead of treating it as an isolated unique case, the amorous relationship between these two characters becomes a model. At the same time, it is inscribed in a historical, social, political, and moral context. The love which Lupe feels for a woman whom she defines as a "buga, a woman who apparently has sexual relations only with men" (110) is what leavens the exchange on gender difference and sexual identification between the various dialogists. In this novel lesbianism, and by extension all social and sexual relationships between women, are no longer fictionalized subversively, nor do they form part of the unspeakable, the undescribable, the inassimilable. They exceed the limits of the clandestine and the furtive. The narrator, by resorting very rarely to interior monologues, invites us to surpass the individual subjective aspect of this experience and to better understand the concept of libidinal heterogeneity. In this way the hermeticism and semantic closure in which the theme of lesbianism is circumscribed in Mexican literature is denied. The text is no longer constituted, as in the case of *El diario de José Toledo* or *Las púberes canéforas*, around textual and narrative ambivalences and subversions. In the present story, the word "lesbian" is successfully extracted from the sphere of the unspeakable, at the same time as the common pejorative use of words like butch, dyke, queer, and so forth, is denounced, terms created to name in a ridiculous and denigrating way that "unspeakable." What is not explained gives birth to unfavorable ideas coined in words that permeate common usage. Guadalupe combats the dissemination of erroneous ideas and the ridicule of lesbianism. One must remember that the very word lesbian bears centuries of condemnation. While lesbianism was explained and tolerated in the context of Aeolian woman, it became the object of derision for Attic comedians eager to stiffle and neutralize the feminist movement of the Attic women. The model of emancipation of women of Lesbos illustrated by the poet Sappho disturbed the Attic men, who took up the task of slandering them. The women of Lesbos became "lesbians" and by extension women who practiced homosexuality. It is worth noting here that the identification of feminism with lesbianism and vice versa is problematic in the discussion of questions common to each. This is one of the aspects debated in *Amora*, which finds its origins in Attic comedy.[5] In the minds of many Mexican men and women alike, lesbianism and feminism are still seen as being synonymous.[6] *Amora* seeks to eradicate the systematic linking, the cause and effect relationship which is a product of a conditioned popular imagination. This explains the heterogeneity of the novel's characters, a heterogeneity paradigmatic of the desire to present a range of possibilities: lesbian feminists, lesbians, heterosexual feminists, heterosexuals, feminists, and bisexuals.

Syncrisis, Anacrisis or the Dialecticization of Contradictions: Feminism, Love and its Sexualization

As this subheading suggests, the logic between question and answer in conversation demands thought, retrospection, a return/turning upon oneself in order to examine more deeply the problems posed, to modify the ideas that arise around

---

[5]See David M. Halperin, *One Hundred Years of Homosexuality*, and Sue Ellen Case "Classic Drag: The Greek Creation of Female Parts," *Theater Journal* 37.3 (1985): 317–27.

[6]Numerous studies have been written in the U.S. with respect to the history of lesbianism and its linkage with feminism, and the theoretical problems that this brings. Note those of Wendy Clark, "The Dyke, the Feminist and the Devil," *Sexuality: A Reader*, special edition of *Feminist Review* 6 (1987): 201-15; Adrienne Rich *"Compulsory Heterosexuality and Lesbian Experience";* Jill Dolan "Lesbian Subjectivity in Realism: Dragging at the Margins of Structure and Ideology;" *Performing Feminisms,* ed. Sue Ellen Case, 1990, 40-54. In Mexico see among others the essay of Marta Lamas "Freud y las muchachas: 20 años de feminismo."

such problems and even to combine them.[7] The different dialogues between characters give rise to a series of contradictions characteristic of anacrisis, contradictions that each character in Roffiel's novel attempts to undo. Keeping in mind that the very structure of the text invites the reader to participate in the dialogue, I want to point out some of these contradictions emerging from the numerous verbal exchanges, not to denounce them but rather, to draw out contradictions pregnant with theoretical implications.

Though *Amora* begins with the essentialist binarism man/woman, defining men as a "subcategory" and judging them to be contrary to the wellbeing of women, the central issue is that of heterosexual women and their relationships and attitudes toward lesbian women, which brings us to definition of lesbianism itself. Claudia is presented as the epitome of the "buga," having sexual relationships with two men, one single and one married, without finding real satisfaction in either of these relationships. By virtue of also having a relationship with Lupe her nickname is changed: she is no longer a "buga" but a "bicycle, as bisexuals are often called: they have no problems parking. Bicycling can be practiced in cyclical, alternating, or simultaneous fashion" (54). These nicknames, not very different from the ones Lupe denounced, are paradigmatic of the separatism which even lesbians resort to in order to facilitate the process of sexual identification. At the end of *Amora*, however, Lupe recognizes the sterility of this type of labelling. The problems brought on by her relationship with Claudia and the verbalization of these difficulties lead her to propose something like a manifesto of tolerance. She proposes a struggle against jealousy, possessiveness, unbridled passion, and resentment, and advocates honesty, freedom, and privacy. She invites lesbians who repeat the patterns of domination so common in heterosexual amorous relationships to love in a different way: "We need to learn to love another way: without cutting our wrists, without threatening to jump off a bridge onto the highway, puking in Garibaldi square or stealing a girlfriend's lover so everyone sees how tough I am" (33–34). This theoretical exposition or declaration with respect to her position on the theme of relationships is the product of heated, emotional, and stormy debates. This manifesto, however, does not

[7]For a reflection on the concept of "philosophical conversation" the book edited by Diane P. Michelfeder and Richard E. Palmer, *Dialogue and Deconstruction: The Gadamer-Derrida Encounter,* is useful. In these essays several critics, basing themselves on the exchange between Gadamer and Derrida, between hermeneutics and deconstruction, ponder the different ways of conceiving dialogue and the notion of "vigilance against the pretense of knowledge."

erase some of the affirmations found in the text, nor the textual strategies which help to shape essentialisms on the one hand and on the other to elude the problematic surrounding sexual desire.

In effect, I postulate that in its attempt to destroy what Butler calls "the ideal or image of the coherent heterosexual ideal" (*Bodies That Matter* 122), the story replaces this ideal for another essentialism, that of the lesbian utopia. In a novel in which, according to the Bakhtinian tradition, a style and a "vocabulary of vocality" is emphasized, the presence of the poetic mode with its monological tendency is rare. We observe, however, that two chapters do seem marked by an erotic lyricism through which feminine beauty and grace, passionate tenderness, perfect communion between two female bodies—Claudia's and Lupe's—in the sexual act, are celebrated. These few lyrical passages attract particular attention by their strategic placement in the narration. The first, "Surely the goddesses must love like this," is located approximately at the midpoint of the novel, and it follows the chapter describing the rape of a friend, Rosa María. It appears again in the same fashion after the description of another rape. The centrality and aestheticization of the lesbian sexual encounter operates as a counterpoint to the horror, panic, and repulsion that surrounds the description of the crime. For example:

> He penetrated her from the front and in back, he bit her breasts almost to the point of ripping off her nipples, and the same with her ears. Marta screamed. . . . When he finally ejaculated, Marta tried to get up to put on her clothes, but with a shove he threw her back on the bed.
>
> What do you think, you fucking bitch, that we're done? Well you're wrong, you're staying right here with me some more, don't you see we're having a great time? He hit her some more. He stuck his penis up her ass and then in her mouth.
>
> Take it, eat your own shit, come on, that's all women know how to do: eat shit. Come on, whore, open wide, suck it good, you fucking whore. (27–28)

> Water from the moon, fresh, with silver points. A lace bedsheet. . . . I let the afternoon undress you, consecrate your skin. . . . Your cave of flesh. Yearning, I'm yearning for your mound, the coral between your thighs. . . . I look at you a thousand times. So much moisture runs over us. . . . Come, we're going to love and love and love, and never stop loving. How tenderness shines in your eyes. How your back trembles, arched. So much plenitude in a simple glance. . .

> . Desire overflows in an infinite pendulum swing. Our caresses disperse the night. (71)

While the only description of heterosexual activity is characterized by cruelty, violence, monstrosity, and rape, the lesbian encounter is synonymous with ecstasy, rapture of the senses, excitement, and plenitude both moral and physical. It implies that lesbian sexuality is necessarily joyous, while heterosexual relationships prevent their participants from finding pleasure. By limiting heterosexuality to a frustrated, violent, and humiliating libidinal experience from which women can escape only by opting for a lesbian sexuality, we are led to believe that pleasure for women is impossible outside a lesbian relationship. To a certain degree, *Amora* seems to suggest that all women are lesbians but don't know it by virtue of having been repressed in the course of their erotic and sexual journey. Describing her relationship with Claudia, Lupe explains that "there is an obvious mutual enamoredness, but with no awareness on Claudia's part" (54). As Lupe suggests, this could be due to the cultural conditioning which imprisons Claudia. Nevertheless, even though Claudia opens Roffiel's novel by proclaiming "men are a subcategory" she later adds "but there are some subcategories that I like" (9). This affirmation on Claudia's part is what Lupe endeavors to ignore.

Lupe hopes to reestablish equilibrium, to eradicate the characteristic monolithicism of heterosexuality and to affirm plurality and difference as embodied in the diverse possibilities of sexual expression. Hence the fact that scattered throughout the text isolated affirmations, such as "some guys are OK, some are really beautiful" (41) are found. These statements, however, appear somewhat forced as concessions by Lupe who, hoping to avoid the primary antagonism or the binary opposition Man/Woman, reaffirms exactly the system she hopes to dismantle. She falls into the same kind of reductionism that established the heterosexual model, but in reverse. Lupe and her friends advocated hybridity and reconciliation of difference, but they are unbending with the "bugas." Though she admits at the end of *Amora* that being a woman does not imply an identity in common, the narrative's development is indicative of the desire that it be so.

She insists on the idea of sex between women as the panacea for their sexual frustration: "there are no frigid women, only incompetent men" (58), Lupe declares. Such a statement echoes that of Mexican poet Elías Nandino, who in his collection of poems *Al rojo blanco* asserted that "there are no impotent men, only incompetent women" (25) Is there a way out of this vicious circle? As we saw in Barbachano Ponce and in Blanco, misogyny and the power of the patriarchal system gives rise to male essentialism. Lupe falls at the extreme end, at the same time denouncing male secular predominance. The way in which Claudia's attraction toward Lupe is explained, like many lesbian relationships, is found in what Butler determines as "the logic of repudiation," the result of a defense mechanism which starts up to alleviate an amorous disillusion. Butler explains what she means by the logic of repudiation as follows:

> a lesbian is one who must have had a bad experience with men, or who has not yet found the right one. These diagnoses presume that lesbianism is acquired by virtue of some failure in the heterosexual machinery, thereby continuing to install heterosexuality as the "cause" of lesbian desire; lesbian desire is figured as the fatal effect of a derailed heterosexual causality. (*Bodies That Matter* 127)

What again appears to be glossed over in this novel is the notion of sexual desire. In numerous instances Claudia tries to demonstrate that she is not a stable sexual subject and, whether out of fear or out of conviction, she chooses to admit her bisexuality without defining herself as either heterosexual or "pure" lesbian. The fact that Claudia prefers not to choose between being a "buga" or a lesbian, and that she opts for "bicycling," is precisely what Lupe and her friends question most. For the latter, there is no doubt that Claudia's indecision is due to the inheritance of centuries of heterosexual education. Lupe, confronting the possibility of losing Claudia completely, resigns herself to accepting Claudia's ambivalence, and she admits unwillingly that "she has the right to find herself one hell of a mate" and that "there are men who can be saved" (124).

Nevertheless, the constant reference to heterosexuality leads, as Butler reminds us, to "yet another set of displacements: of desire, of phantasmatic pleasures, and of forms of love that are not reducible to a heterosexual matrix and the logic of repudiation" (*Bodies That Matter* 127). Throughout the conversations between Lupe and her friends, the idea that being a woman is a pleasure is reiterated. What does the notion of pleasure refer to in the realm of intimate relationships between two women? According to the text, pleasure consists of relating socially and affectively with other women, thus fleeing from contact with a person of the other sex. Lupe and the other women conceive of and take pleasure in their relationships, through the rich friendship that they have developed, through every-day contact, telephone conversations, the exchange of letters, the books they discuss, the dinners, the cafés, the laughter. The "zero communication, the terrible sex, the rampant narcissism of men and the slow wearing down that this brings to women" (110) are contraposed to the idea that "it would be easier to build an amorous relationship between two women because there is more communication, less fear of commitment, more compromise, more identification" (113). Identification with whom? In the same way that "heterosexual logic requires identification and desire to be mutually exclusive" (Butler, *Bodies That Matter* 240), De Lauretis states that "to desire a woman does not necessarily imply an identification with her female gender" (24). But precisely in order to understand this, one would have to escape the logic of repudiation and the heterosexual referential system. Discussion of the notion of sexual desire would be needed. Little is said in the novel of the sexualization of amorous relationships. While men are "interested first in sex," women "care about getting to know each other first and sex comes later;" besides the fact that the proliferation of cliches preserves the characteristic binary opposition of heterosexuality, it is a posture that goes against feminist efforts to reestablish the right of women to define themselves sexually according to their own rules. Norma, for example, explains her sexuality without broaching the subject of desire: "It's not the solution nor the panacea. But at least with women I don't have to be on the defensive, I don't feel like a sex object, they don't rape me" (45). In this quote explaining her sexual relationships with other women, it is noteworthy that the desire she feels for these women is not expressed, there is an absence of erotic libido. Her lesbian relationships correspond rather to the need to construct a restricted and therefore safe space where the phallus has no place. This reaction is understandable in the sense that it is opposed to the patriarchal economy. It raises several important questions so as to not trivialize the historical oppression and victimization of the "feminine" in heterosexual and homosexual relationships. First, this type of affirmation keeps both male and female sexuality imprisoned within social models that the Law of the Father has established: male sexuality is, as a result, necessarily aggressive, and female sexuality is seen as being passive and complacent. This polarization between men and women finally denies women the possibility of choosing the type of sexuality they want to "practice" within the multiplicity of ways of administering their sexuality and their erotic identities. This type of polarization also seems to avoid the fact that gender, social and psychological "appearance" in no way guarantees an "equal" erotic and amorous relationship. This could even run counter to the erotic fantasies of many women. This problem is further complicated when, in an effort to define lesbian identity, she denounces "women who want a lot of sex. They're not lesbians, they're machos with a vagina" (112). The sexual "aggressiveness"[8] of these women is

[8]The need to associate women with "monstrosity" has formed part of many cultures throughout the centuries. Writer and essayist Sergio González Rodríguez reminds us, in his study of erotic or pornographic literature prohibited in Mexico

denounced: wanting and having many sexual partners goes against the utopian and romantic eroticism that lesbian sexuality is identified with in *Amora*. Lesbian sexuality is not only good and satisfying because it provides a "safe" space, but also because it excludes the possibility of "a lot of sex" from the lesbian economy, a negative privilege of the male domain: a lot of sex is bad and a little sex is good. Lesbian amorous relationships are harmonious and "healthy" when this relationship begins with a "profound awareness of the other, and the sexual comes later, as a logical consequence. With guys everything starts with the physical" (64). Being lesbian appears to be reduced to having little sex, few sexual fantasies, because the contrary would be equivalent to recreating the heterosexual male model. But the idea that the world of women's sexual fantasies is "natural" and biologically limited corresponds to one of the most damaging myths created by the patriarchal system, to deny women the possibility of their own eroticism. According to the model proposed in the novel, the lesbian woman is not allowed to choose the conditions of her own sexuality or to define what constitutes for her individually a sensual adventure, the arousal of both physical and intellectual senses, and it keeps alive the stereotyping of eroticism on which the heterosexual system is based.[9] Besides excluding from the lesbian community those lesbians who want "a lot of sex" and defining them as "machos with a vagina," it denies

---

during the first three decades of this century, that "the taste for horrifying women at the end of the nineteenth and the twentieth centuries, for Medusas, women-children, Sphinxes, Lesbians, Sirens, Harpies, and Vampires, in whom the risky pleasures of decapitating Judith or Salome lurked, represents the terrible image of woman which man constructed when the former began to play a new role in the modern world" (31).

[9]On the problem of the relationship between "sexual gender" and the question of sexuality, the following works are particularly interesting: Gayle Rubin, "Thinking Sex: Notes for a Radical Theory of the Politics of Sexuality," *Pleasure and Danger,* ed. Carol Vance, 1984, 267-320; Ruby Rich "Feminism and Sexuality in the 1980's," *Feminist Studies* 12:3 (1986): 525-61; Catherine McKinnon, *Feminism Unmodified: Discourses on Life and Law,* 1987; Sue Ellen Case, "Towards a Butch-Femme Aesthetic," *Making a Spectacle,* ed. Lynda Hart, 1989; Jill Dolan, "The Dynamics of Desire: Sexuality and Gender in Pornography and Performance," *Theater Journal* 39:2 (1987): 157-74; Joan Nestle "The Fem Question," *Pleasure and Danger*, ed. Carol Vance; Carol S. Vance, "Pleasure and Danger: Toward a Politics of Sexuality"; Ann Snitow et al., *The Powers of Desire: The Politics of Sexuality 1983;* and the works of Judith Butler, *Gender Trouble,* 1990 and *Bodies that Matter*, 1993.

the possibility of repeated and plural erotic "conversations" between two women, and maintains the oppositional reference to the heterosexual economy for the purposes of definition. This gives rise to a homogenous conception of lesbianism which privileges the "femme" lesbian relationship.[10]

"No guy gives me what you do, but I'm not a lesbian." With this declaration, Claudia poses a fundamental question: what does it mean to be a lesbian? As discussed above, this novel proposes definitions that are debatable because of the arguments they are founded on. The exclusion of "machos with a vagina" points to the reductive aspect on which these definitions are based. As Butler explains, these definitions are founded on "the threat that compels the assumption of masculine and feminine attributes. . . ." For the man, the adoption of feminine attributes is synonymous with the "descent into female castration and abjection," and for the woman the adoption of male attributes is synonymous with a "monstrous ascent into phallicism" (*Bodies That Matter* 103). This process gives birth to what Butler herself calls "figures of homosexual abjection," such as the feminized fag and the phallicized dyke (*marimacha*). These figures of abjection or "inverted versions of heterosexualized masculinity and femininity" (103) are those used most frequently in the heterosexual economy to ridicule both male and female homosexuality. In the same manner, the dyke represents in this novel the abject figure of female homosexuality in order to avoid establishing a link between the formation of a lesbian identity and heterosexuality. Thus, in order to establish an appearance of identity specific to the group and specifically characteristic of it, it is necessary to reject heterosexuality. Butler concludes convincingly that this way of proceeding "attribute[s] a false unity to heterosexuality, but it misses the political opportunity to . . . refute the logic of mutual exclusion by which heterosexism proceeds" (*Bodies That Matter* 113). We would add that not

---

[10]Mexican anthropologist and journalist Marta Lamas, in her study "Freud y las muchachas", objects to this type of one-sided representation. She alludes to a lesbianism of "overflowing diversity": "there were lesbians of all types and after a time it was recognized that the fact of being lesbian, in and of itself, did not explain or guarantee anything. On the way disagreements and confrontations also arose. The lesbians of the past were suspicious of women who "converted" to lesbianism for political reasons and were aggressive towards them. There were others who, recognizing the complexity of desire, entered into sadomasochistic practices and defended their position against "femme" lesbians for whom love between women was always rose-colored. The discomfort and ambivalence of other feminists confronted with the "butch" vs."femme" debate reflected their own contradictory positions on this violent aspect of sexuality" (71–72).

only does it attribute a false unity to heterosexuality, but also to homosexuality and in this case to lesbianism. Most critics agree that repudiating heterosexuality is a step that allows "sexual minorities" to mark their difference and to initiate the process of identification with said difference. Nevertheless, these identities are constructed through oppositions and rejections, which leads to the prescription of "an exclusive identification for a multiply constituted subject" (Butler, *Bodies That Matter* 116).

What gives rise to or initiates the debate between Lupe and her friends is precisely the urgent need she feels to eradicate the notion of uniform identity. By insisting on the notion of coherence in the formation of group identity, she falls, however, into the same reductionism against which she initially struggled. On several occasions Claudia is accused of "polygamy," for being unable to choose between her male lovers and Lupe, for her lack of solidarity, care, and respect. Her bisexuality is reproached for being, according to Lupe, a way of avoiding commitment and especially the social stigma which the label of lesbian brings. Being bisexual is not considered as a possible reaction to the rigidity of the heterosexual system (and by extension here that of lesbianism), as a manifestation of the fluidity of the sexual subject; it is seen as a betrayal of lesbianism. Butler warns us of the danger of reading bisexuality this way, since this logic, according to her, "is reiterated in the failure to recognize bisexuality as well as in the normativizing interpretation of bisexuality as a failure of loyalty or lack of commitment—two cruel strategies of erasure" (*Bodies That Matter* 112).

The problems posed in this novel around the conceptualization of lesbian sexual identity are due in part to the way in which the dialogue is developed. If, as stated at the beginning of this chapter, Roffiel's novel is one accessible to a majority through the conversational style that characterizes it, then it can easily become a pedagogical "tool." To a certain degree it recalls the method Plato utilized in the last period of his life which consisted of forming and educating neophytes.[11] There is no doubt that Roffiel endeavors to instruct using the

---

[11]Bakhtin explains that in Plato's last works, Socrates becomes a "teacher" and the "monologism of the content begins to destroy the form of Socratic dialogue. Therefore when the genre of Socratic dialogue enters the service of established and dogmatic points of view in the worldview of various philosophical schools and religious doctrines, it loses its connection with the carnivalesque sense of the world and is transformed into a mere form for expounding what had already been discovered, irrefutable ready-made truths. In the end it degenerates completely into a form of questions and answers for instructing neophytes" (*Problems* 110).

literary form. In my opinion this didactic method helps to produce the essentialisms studied earlier, and it privileges certain bodies of explanation and postures. Pedagogically, to refer even oppositionally to what is already known and assimilated—as is the heterosexual system—is to facilitate the introduction of new material, ideas, and concepts unknown to the neophyte. This provides a referential frame, recognizable markers. At the same time simplifying or enabling entry into the subject, I agree with Butler that "the citing of the dominant norm does not, in this instance, displace that norm" (*Bodies That Matter* 133). On the contrary, it gives the "ignorant" the possibility of retreating to the known and allows him/her to adopt the initial point of reference as a safe base from which to define the object of "learning." If the Socratic system of dialogue is used, rightly or wrongly, toward didactic ends, it does not mean that one can forget its original role: that of "philosophizing" (in the case of this novel, on the formation of different social, political, and sexual identities). The dialogue gives rise to a pluralism of opinions which Gaston Bachelard classifies as "the only method able to inform such diverse elements of experience and of theory" (*La Philosophie* 12). The dialogues, oriented toward discovery, constantly risk the emergence of dualities and hierarchies. Bachelard himself adds that it is precisely "the will to objectivity that leads us to discover the subjective parts that remain in each of us: vague ideas, contradictions, fixed ideas, unproven convictions" (13).

The publication of this novel represents a historical event in Mexico, as it adds to the growing number of novels which, by Bachelard's formula, "set up knowledge as an evolution of the spirit, which accepts the variations that strike against the unity and the perennity of the 'Cogito'" (*La Philosophie* 9). Despite its limitations, which can be attributed to the contentiousness of the debate, Roffiel deploys a language that attempts to represent lesbian desire. She affirms at the same time the importance of novels which aspire to change our consciousness with respect to the literary construction of diverse identities. As was mentioned at the beginning of this chapter, this novel does not resort to subterfuge. It refuses to resort to abstract narration of a concrete reality in order to rescue from oblivion those who form part of that reality. Roffiel expects this text to be read as a feminist lesbian text and she signs it without ambivalence.

The end of *Amora* admits its own duality. It is an ending which attempts to repair or compensate for the presence of essentialist affirmations throughout the text: "Claudia turned out to be a real intensive course" (161). These words echo those of Claudia at the beginning of the novel when she referred to her experience with Lupe as "the university of life." Without a doubt it invites us to learn and practice tolerance. Gadamer wrote that "in every genuine conversation neither the last nor the first word is uttered" (Michelfeder 12). This novel could be read as a "theoretical fiction," a term coined by De Lauretis to describe a "formal, experimental, critical, lyrically autobiographical and theoretically aware practice of writing in the feminine, a practice that aspires to overrun gender boundaries" (*Sexual* 165).

CHAPTER 7: *TODO ESTÁ PERMITIDO,* OR THE BANALIZATION OF TRANSGRESSION

Todo está permitido (*Everything is Allowed,* 1994), Oscar de la Borbolla's second novel, is defined in the cover of the book as "a daring an erotic story that narrates the entertaining sexual adventures of a woman (Gabriela) in search of success and satisfaction." But this novel also distinguishes itself for its extravagance, excess, dissoluteness, lubricity, perversion since its main character, Gabriela, drags us unashamedly into the most elicitory erogenous zones. Borbolla's novel belongs to a genre, the Mexican erotic tale, scarcely included among canonical literature and whose life "is as stormy as the frictions caused by the tension between modern changes and the burden of tradition" (González Rodríguez 31). With this novel Borbolla joins the order of what Mexican critic and writer González Rodríguez calls "the conspiracy of the erotics." According to him, this conspiracy was gestated around 1893 with the publication of José Juan Tablada's poem "Fisa negra."[1]

Borbolla's novel could be seen by certain critics as an anomaly in this age of political correctness that characterizes our decade, as a "folly." Borbolla's "madness" in this novel is double: first, for creating a character who does not seem so different from the nineteenth-century pornographic novel's typical heroine, who introduces us to the vicissitudes of social enhancement by entering the illicit business of prostitution, and sexual pleasure; second, for creating a narrator whose sexual fantasies hinge upon uncontrollable desires rather than upon politically correct compulsion. Madness for competing with Federico Gamboa's Santa, the most famous prostitute in Mexican literature, and for generating a text that seems to be controlled by male fantasies at a time when Mexican feminists struggle physically and theoretically "so that the textual and erotic body does not exclusively follow the contour of a female body that remains the object of an atavistic male ignorance" (Glantz 115).

In this chapter I wish to raise several fundamental questions. Is *Todo está permitido* an erotic or pornographic novel? How useful is it to distinguish

---

[1]The Printing Law of 1917 issued by Venustiano Carranza's government censored Tablada's erotic tales and those of his followers (*Intermedios* 31).

such categories?[2] Octavio Paz in his book *La llama doble. Amor y erotismo*, asserts that "eroticism is a socialized sexuality transfigured by men's imagination and volition" (14). Could we define pornography in the same manner? When Paz speaks of men's imagination and volition is he refering to *man-hui* anthropos/nonspecified gender (to use Hélène Cixous's formulation)? This ambiguity is in fact the major problem when it comes to defining eroticism and pornography, that is, the exclusion of women as subjects governing their bodies and pleasures. Should we read Borbolla's novel as a reiteration of familiar cliches which seem to have characterized and dominated erotic accounts? Are the characters and their narrator moving beyond the spectacle of sexuality and the production of sexual fantasies true to traditional erotic/pornographic representations?

Very few studies have been devoted in Mexico to the historicization and the fictionalization of the question of pornography, prostitution and eroticism. The work of Sergio González Rodríguez is an exception. His introduction to *Los amores: relatos eróticos mexicanos* (*Lovers: Erotic Mexican Tales*, 1993), and *Los bajos fondos* (*Underworld*, 1989) stand out because they trace the evolution of cultural and sexual marginality in Mexico City. In *Los amorosos*, González Rodríguez examines the crucial role that the many moralizing campaigns played in the genesis of sexual marginality and its underworld from the Porfirian period until today. The question of public morality has preocupied Mexican institutions since the colonial times. The independence process did not alter the status quo when it came to dealing with such taboo issues as prostitution and pornography. The urbanization of Mexico City reinforced, between 1867–1917, the different governments's sanitization efforts. During the 1920s and 1930s these efforts became increasingly institutionalized with the enactment of sanitary measures through the Penal Code of 1931 and the Sanitary Code of 1935:

---

[2]In her article "Sexing the Bildungsroman: Las edades de Lulú," Silvia Bermúdez also points to "the subjective nature between "erotica" and "pornography" and calls on Ralph Ginzburg statement of 1959: "no truly satisfactory definition of erotica (and/or pornography or obscenity) has ever been devised. The concept is entirely too subjective." Bermúdez adds that "almost thirty years later the topic remains as entangled as ever, and no amount of clarification seems to untie the knots of confusion. According to Elizabeth Cowie, when debating the issue of pornography there is a confusion arising from, among other things, "the attempt to distinguish between permissible sexual imagery and 'pornography,' where the permissible imagery is variously claimed as 'erotic' or 'art' or 'socially redeeming' in contrast to 'pornography'" (qtd. by Bermúdez).

> In its article 200, the Penal Code determines what constitutes a felony against public morality and decency and punishes from six months to five years in jail with fines up to 10000 pesos anyone who would fabricate, reproduce or publish books, writings, images or obscene objects, and anyone who would expose, distribute or circulate them. . . . As for the Sanitary Code it dealt with the problem of prostitution. However, one had to wait until 1940 for the practice of the "abolitionist system" to be enforced in Mexico City. (*Bajos fondos* 33)

The witch hunt intensified in 1940 as morality and decency were considered essential to national unity and progress. The search for public health still justifies today the many campaigns of censorship prohibiting, among other things, "erotic publications and in 1990, the Penal Code penalized pornography. Yet the constant political and moral repression did not prevent the clandestine dissemination of publications considered "barbarous pornography" from coming to Mexico mainly via Spain between 1890 to 1930 (*Bajos fondos* 55; see also the "Anexos" in *Los amorosos* pages 403–10). In 1985, for instance, in spite of the censorship, Mexico witnessed an explosion of "clandestine" and erotic publications which coincided with the wider approbation of sexual and erotic matters among Mexicans living in urban settings.

Many well-known writers since Federico Gamboa have penetrated the insalubrious literary realm of sexual desire and lust. This distinguished group of writers include such figures as Alfonso Reyes, Salvador Novo, José Revueltas, Salvador Elizondo, Juan García Ponce, Inés Arredondo, Sergio Pitol, Carlos Fuentes, Fernando del Paso, Sergio Galindo, José Agustín, and many others. Among the younger generation of writers, we find the erotic vein in the work of Angeles Mastretta, Sara Levi Calderón, Luis Zapata, Hector Aguilar Camín, Enrique Serna, to name a few, and of course one of the most red-handed erotic writer, Oscar de la Borbolla.

Is *Todo está permitido* a pornographic novel? The answer is probably yes. Before delving into the different studies that attempt to define the term "pornography," we would first like to examine how Borbolla manipulates the semantic roots of the word pornography and to what end. The word pornography comes from the Greek *pornê* for prostitution and from *graphos* for discourse. Borbolla emphasizes not only pornography in his novel as "a coincidence of sexual phantasy, genre and culture in an erotic organization of visibility" (Beverly Brown's definition of pornography in Williams 269), but also as a coincidence of prostitution and political and social discourse in Mexico. If as Foucault put it, "madness is the name that a culture attributes to an exteriority that it rejects," (564) Borbolla's madness lies in the ostentatious, insolent, and lustful fictionalization of those "exteriorities."

Gabriela, a "sex-worker," finds pleasure while charging for it. But her pleasure also derives from her exploiting a kind of institutionalized prostitution that prevails in Mexican politics and society at large at the same time she embodies the multiple exteriorities that this same culture rejects: First as a prostitute, that is to say as a traditional public woman who both morality and a certain group of feminists anathematize (although for different reasons), and second as the character who will demystify phallocratic power. With this character, Borbolla transgresses official morality by pointing to its obscenity and its "social disorder" through the apparent "sexual disorder" of the novel (I borrow Bataille's formulation here).

In many ways *Todo está permitido* works as an "asylary space" where the lubric narrator "needs to admit his guilt and to free himself from it, to allow the truth of his illness to surface and then to eliminate it, to take up with his freedom again alienating it in the doctor's volition" (Foucault 547). The narrator's guilt lies, on the one hand, in giving free rein to male fantasies (considered to be perverse madness for many radical feminists) and, on the other hand, in defying and mocking one of the most deeply-rooted "national" characteristics, that is, corruption and male chauvinism (*machismo*). By eliminating this double pathology he takes up with his freedom, although alienating it first in the will of radical feminists and second in the will of Mexican phallocratic *machismo*. If, as French anthropologist Maurice Godelier suggested, "sexuality always speaks of something and somewhere else as well as it evinces something else than sex, and if the erotic scene is the symbolic expression of a social and political order of which the woman's body is the marquing terrain" (in Hans and Lapouge 169), Borbolla's novel could precisely be resemanticizing this terrain, dismantling the patriarchal system that circumscribes it. In order to express his madness Borbolla creates an "autonomous language," what Foucault defined as a "lyricism of *folie*" since "discourse [here Borbolla's discourse] is common to delirium and to dream and to the possibility of a lyricism of desire and of a poetry of the world that find themselves joined together" (536). Foucault adds that "madness and dream are at once the moment of extreme subjectivity and of ironic objectivity" (536). Hence the fact that Borbolla's novel operates as a double movement of alienation/perversion and of parody/liberation that "points to the presence of other times and places coexisting in time and space, drawing attention to the chaotic way in which the mad person breaks the apparent order of things" (*Ucronías* 139).

In what follows I would like to delve further into the definitions frequently abscribed to the word pornography and eroticism. If we were to subscribe to the definitions given to those two terms by the *Dictionary of the Royal Academy* of Spain, that is that pornography "is a treatise on prostitution" and a pornographer "a person who writes on prostitution," the novel would, without any doubt, be pornographic and Borbolla and his narrator, pornographers. I would rather base my analysis on the broader definitions provided by the French dictionary *Le Grand Robert* and by the *Webster's New World Dictionary*. In the *Robert* the definitions of eroticism and pornography emphasize the idea of the licentious, of the punishable excess in the enjoyment of sexual pleasures. While the *Webster* does not make mention of the issue of chastisement when defining pornography and its "depiction of erotic behavior intended to cause sexual excitement," it pairs eroticism, as does the *Robert*, with pathology. Pornography, on the other hand, is often defined as the representation of sexual or obscene matters which implies "to bring clearly before the mind," and for the *Robert* "to bring clearly before the mind and the eye," "to sensitize by means of an image," "or to evoke and to stage" these matters. Eroticism could then be the noble, more abstract, and less stigmatized term that is given to anything related in one way or another to carnal pleasures. This could explain the fact that French critic and writer Anne Marie Dardigan defines eroticism "as a hoax of which women are the victims" (Hans and Lapouge 173). To this I would like to add that in terms of visual and verbal representation, eroticism is not that different from pornography but, I would contend, its alibi.

What seems to distance these two concepts, however, is the issue of representation: eroticism limits itself to being an inclination for sexually related matters which does not necessarely imply the practice, the written or visual evocation of this predilection. Generally, the fictionalization of female sexual pleasure in pornographic and erotic texts is characterizedby a coercive and traditional male intervention. This is what radical feminists object to; this critique is founded on the indiscriminate equation made between eroticism and pornography. In *Todo está permitido*, Borbolla follows in the footsteps of libertine Mexican writers but also in those of established European libertines such as the Marquis de Sade, Georges Bataille, and Pierre Klossowski. André Gide wrote that "the dissolute's biggest pleasure is to corrupt." While Borbolla attempts to define, albeit parodically, an ontology that explores all the conceivable possibilities while exhausting sexual pleasure, the narrator, Gabriela, and the reader should live in excess and transfigure eroticism into a true asceticism. The aims of the narrator in this novel are to corrupt and to eroticize with its lubric orgies, first its characters, and then, its readers. As in Georges Bataille's *Madame Edwarda* or as in Sade's *Justine* where the erotic myth always ends up as a *mise en scè-*

ne—be it gestural or theatrically figurative—in *Todo está permitido* one can observe "a taste for disguise, for a theatrical process, and where the erotic scene becomes a place of theatrical concentrations. The disguise, this representation, is necessary to establish a distance from the staging of the sexual act" (Dardigna in Hans and Lapouge 168). In Borbolla's novel everything is a pretext to staging/representing performances in which parodic exaggerations and libidinal excess border on the Foucauldian "lyricism of *folie*" alluded to earlier. This is particularly true of the chapters which introduce the reader to the "plays" staged in the brothel where Gabriela works, to the clients' performances of their fantasies, or even to those plays which stage the shows that Gabriela requires from her masseurs while staying at a resort in Cancún. Moreover, the "red sweater" that accompanies Gabriela during crucial moments of her life, this disguise *par excellence,* becomes the indispensable amulet-fetish for her seductive enterprise.

However, Borbolla does not merely reproduce traditional pornographic/erotic literature's distinctive and recognizable features. Instead, he sets out to redefine its characteristics in order to reinvent the genre. For one thing, Borbolla's novel does not aim to confront the angst that comes with the erotic performance as evident in Bataille's or Sade's texts, nor to rival them in licentiousness. If eroticism presents itself in the novel as "disorder," it is not the kind of disorder that aligns itself with, for instance, Bataille's thanatos. Everything is eros in *Todo está permitido*. If, as Maurice Blanchot asserts, Sade's books such as *Justine et Juliette* "remain a secret, a work perfectly unreadable, unreadable because of its length, its composition, and its repetitions . . . a book that nobody can make public" (18), Borbolla's novel aims to be public and accessible to all. While for Sade only one law prevails, one's own pleasure and egotistic eroticism embracing the belief that "the equality of human beings rests in the right to equally use all human beings for one's own ends" (Blanchot 20), Borbolla offers a revisionist alternative to the notion of equality and eroticism. Likewise, Borbolla does not amalgamate/fuse pornography/eroticism with sadism and violence (which has been the major cause of discord between feminists and pornographers). Neither are women the victims of the humor, as in Sade's work, that characterizes each erotic scene, their descriptions, or the many puns present in the novel. Chapter VIII, for instance, is an obvious parody of the circle of excrement that enthralled writers such as Pier Paolo Pasolini and Sade. It is a parody of the sacralization of the excrement and of some pornographers' scatological obsession in their search for a more cerebral sexuality. It is also a parodic wink to the long tradition established by Aristophanes and his followers who continue to associate prostitution with the excremental. Therefore, Gabriela becomes a "hermeneut of shit," as Borbolla puts it, an oracle of excrement, a very unrefined one whose motivation is far removed from a ferocious fascination with the object of study.

Another example of the parody can be found in the chapters where one of Gabriela's Madames is producing, in her brothel, the erotic fantasy of an oil tycoon from the Middle East. The theatralization of sex reaches epic proportions. The tycoon, who is fascinated with ostriches, is ready to pay astronomical amounts of money to "make out" with four hundred prostitutes disguised as ostriches and whose heads should be buried in holes made into the platform of an immense stage as their rears are up: "The work sounded easy: the four hundred prostitutes only had to hide their heads in the platform, hold their buttocks adorned with feathers up, and scream when the tycoon penetrated them" (94–95). By dedicating these pages to the representation of this "bestial" fantasy, Borbolla enters, dauntlessly, the realm of the ultimate hedonic taboo. Yet he manages to preserve the outlawed, the unpermissible, while demystifying the issue of bestiality and sex by means of a hilariously wild narration of the whole event. The episode also pokes fun at the cabaret culture in Mexico City.

Oscar de la Borbolla uses humor as Freud did, as "something that is not only liberating but also sublime and elevated" although without sacralizing or objectifying the female character. Many feminist readers will be tempted to denounce a spectacle, no matter how humorous, that grounds itself in the gaze of a male reader and a male narrator. One can not deny the fact that the narrator is the epitome of the "voyeur." He wallows, shamelessly, in the pleasure of watching Gabriela during her most intimate and private moments without being seen. Linda Williams in her influential book *Hard Core, Power, Pleasure, and the Frenzy of the Visible* reminds us that "in most pornography, the woman's body is solicited, questioned, and probed for secrets that are best revealed when herself is not in control" (51).

However, in *Todo está permitido*, and this is where lies the originality of the novel, there is an attempt to give control back to the female character. The penises in the novel do not rule: most of them are "deflated" and in their detumescence they fail to symbolize phallic power. Borbolla does not hope to castrate with his novel half of Mexico, but rather to parody the idea of unlimited virility and those men who place their power in their "fly." The narrator does not conceal his male fantasies nor does he hide the fact that Gabriela's body stages his erotic imaginary. Yet he intervenes in his narration in order to rectify this atavic fallacy, his literary and sexual construction, the "nymph of his red soul," allowing Gabriela to gain back control over the erotic spectacle:

> Gabriela began to moan, caressing her breasts and when it seemed she was about to come, she looked in my direction, I mean outside of her

> story... But, to where was Gabriela really looking? Toward the transparent dome of her bathroom from where I was contemplating her, toward the wet tip of my pen of which each letter was whirling water round her body? No: Gabriela was not looking at anything; she was seeing without seeing, as it always happens during an orgasm . . . and when I thought to be reaching the dome of this page, she stopped, and with her eyes disappearing behind the soap, she streched out her arm and turned off the jacusi. (111)

In this steamy passage, Borbolla allows Gabriela the literary or narrative power to interrupt his fantasy and orgasm. He allows her to hold the narrator's "pen" and to redirect it, driving it to write a different kind of ending to this erotic scene, an ending that shuts the narrator off her orgasmic realm . The erotic woman is here legitimate and Gabriela has little in common with the pathos that characterized Santa in Gamboa's novel. Here libidinal excess does not correspond only to male discourse narrating female sexuality to other men. Gabriela is presented as a young woman whose sexual emancipation is also possible in lust. The narrator does everything possible to minimize his interventions, although it is sometimes a difficult, even impossible, task. However, the process of self-rehabilitation of self-censorship, no matter how painstaking, has been initiated. He might not be able to eliminate his fantasy, yet he does not pretend it is anything else but a fantasy. Moreover, who says that being looked at is something that women systematically reject? Williams laments the fact that by posing this question radical feminists consider us as accomplices of a misogynist economy. Essentialism brings certain feminists to think that this kind of pleasure is itself completely conditionned by masculine definitions of pleasure. I agree with Williams that it is difficult, for some women, to acknowledge the sexual excitement that texts such as Borbolla's can elicit in feminist readers like us. As Williams explains, however, the position of these radical feminists is as controlling as the one of a man narrating the female body to other men, since they are also dictating what defines pleasure.

In her valuable and audacious reevaluation of hard-core pornography, Williams affirms that

> pornography produced by women, for instance, offer spaces where people, specially women, can enact their desires without fear of punishment, guilt, or self-consciousness. . . . Though very different spaces, all are simultaneously safe and exciting places where women can be sexual

without being labeled nymphomaniacs, femmes fatales, or simply bad. (253)

In De la Borbola's novel the narrator's process of self-rehabilitation brings him to also create safe spaces like the ones Williams describes, spaces and situations where Gabriela can indulge in pleasure without being the victim of gratuitous male violence or simply of morality. As mentioned earlier, violence and cruelty do not have a place in this novel and do not seem necessary in order to enter the realm of maddening desire. Safety does not decrease sexual arousal, quite on the contrary.

Another telling example paradigmatic of the process of the narrator's re-education can be found in a passage that will undoubtedly give rise to controversy due to the question of children and sexuality. In this passage the narrator, who dramatizes the lust of two children, one being Gabriela at twelve years old and the other the four-year-old boy she babysits for, does not hide comfortably behind his narration, but rather comes forward, revealing himself and confronting the ambiguity of the desires that bring him to represent this fantasy. Yet he also alters his narration so that the boy's parents (the adult world) do not catch them in the middle of forbidden lovemaking:

> As Gabriela went on with her marbles and her whore-like dance on the bed, I had no choice but to have them take a detour in the novel, so that they could be found in a house identical to theirs, where another Gabriela and another boy had spent a quiet evening watching television . . . and when the parents came out, they kissed their son goodnight . . . not knowing that their real son and the real Gabriela were still at it in the real novel. (26)

This intervention in the course of the narration, this detour, could be read also as a pretext since, while diverting the parents and the readers from such a transgression, the narrator protects his own delirium, his perversion, the perversion of a pedophile who needs to conceal his social and sexual deviation. The narrator looks and obviously narrates not only what he sees but what his fantasy requires him to see. On the other hand, the narrator's intervention helps equate the novelistic space to a safe place, a privileged space where transgression is protected, a locus that does not limit nor condemn children's sexuality and their fictionalization.

In his study *Los bajos fondos* González Rodríguez postulates that

> in terms of social morality, public language and esthetic ideas one can distinguish, since the 70s, two types of literature in México: a diurnal type and a nocturnal type. The diurnal would be the one that evolves within the limits of the conventional, the one that inherits traditions and normal language, without excluding however, momentary and transient incursions in what should not be said. On the contrary, the nocturnal presents an immersion in the abnormal, the proscribed, the exceptional, illicit, illegal. (90)

Borbolla's novel places itself in between these two types of literature or even enters a third category which would undermine and challenge the binome that González Rodríguez conceives; that is to say, a literature that hopes to shed light upon the nocturnal quality of the diurnal and vice versa. Borbolla's novel fuses together these two concepts considering the fact that if the nocturnal opposes itself to the diurnal, the diurnal becomes a nondiurnal, a defective diurnal with negative value attached to it. Therefore the diurnal is what it is by virtue of its negation or its opposition to the nocturnal, as an antithesis so that the total identity of the diurnal becomes endangered. With this logic the diurnal needs the nocturnal in order to affirm itself.

Borbolla points to the incongruency of the binary, to the negativity that infuses the traditional uncoupling and coupling of the nocturnal with the diurnal. Instead, he shows that the nocturnal (understood as the abnormal, proscribed, exceptional, illicit) is not so different from what characterizes the diurnal with its political and social corruption, its hypocrisy and supposed morality. Likewise, the nocturnal can also win back an aura of normality, of regularity without having any of its organs affected by pathological modifications. For Borbolla the nocturnal is as honorable, legitimate, and intelligible as the diurnal (with all the irony this assertion entails). By covering the diurnal with a nocturnal veil and vice versa, Borbolla banalizes both these concepts and the myths surrounding them. He invalidates the taboos attached to the nocturnal as well as the sense of normality that characterizes the diurnal. Neither the diurnal nor the nocturnal can be read through fixed definitions.

Borbolla hopes to banalize the interchangeability between these two terms and what defines them. His novel extends beyond the last page in the sense that it should be reread "after the shock of the new," as Patrice Petro in her article entitled "Aftershock/Between Boredom and History" suggests; that is, "when the shock of the new ceases to be shocking, when change itself has become routinized, commodified, banalized and when the usual, and the fantastic become inextricably linked to the boring, the prosaic, and the everyday" (265).

The "excessive visibility" of sexuality, its "overepresentation" (terms I borrow from Meaghan Morris and her work on banality) and the repetition contribute in this novel to the banalization of sexual transgression. This explains the irreverent tone in the novel which equally aims to the banalization of transgression as well as to be "provocative in its utter banality" (Petro 279).

One should also add, however, that in this novel Borbolla builds a utopian erotic/pornographic world. I also agree with Mexican writer and critic Margo Glantz, that "a good erotic text is built as a utopia" (115). Notwithstanding, Borbolla's novel resembles Charles Woken's mental hospital, which Borbolla himself describes as "a rehabilitation center for normal people, for these healthy people to recover or to develop their benumbed senses, so that they overcome the poorness of these five canals with which they learn about a stunted and narrow world; so that they take a look at the pluridimentional vastness of the unfathomable and vertiginous universe and oppose the imposition of a reality and a definition of reason that are nothing else but the product of an intolerant and impoverished sensorial perception" (*Ucronías* 140).

Some critics would see Borbolla as a traditional Mexican male writer who participates in a masculine discourse on sexuality. Nothing in the narration denies his participation in this type of discourse. Rather, Borbolla shows that it is possible to undermine from within one's own problematic discourse.

BIBLIOGRAPHY

Abbott, Porter H. *Diary Fiction. Writing as Action*. Ithaca: Cornell UP, 1984.

Acevedo, Sybil de, et al. *Auguste Comte "qui êtes vous?"* Lyon: Editions Manufacture, 1988.

Adler de Lomnitz, Larissa. *Cómo sobreviven los marginados*. México, D.F.: Siglo XXI, 1978.

Alighieri, Dante. *The Divine Comedy*. Translated and Edited by John D. Sinclair. New York: Oxford UP, 1961.

Alvarado, Lourdes. *El siglo XIX ante el feminismo: Una interpretación positivista*. México, D.F.: Universidad Nacional Autónoma de México, 1991.

Alvarez, Federico. "José Toledo contra Miguel Barbachano Ponce." *La cultura en México Siempre* 136 (September 23, 1964): xvi–xvii.

Anderson, Danny. "Cultural Studies and Reading Culture in 20th Century Mexico." *Indiana Journal of Hispanic Literatures* 6.7 (Spring–Fall 1995): 207–35.

—. "Reading, Social Control, and the Mexican Soul in *Al filo del agua*." *Mexican Studies* 11 1 (1995): 45–73.

Assouline, Pierre. "Entretien avec Roger Stéphane." *Lire* 206 (November 1992): 18–23.

—. "L'Homosexualité est-elle un atout littéraire"? *Lire* 206 (November 1992): 18–23.

Axthelm, Peter. *The Modern Confessional Novel*. New Haven: Yale UP, 1967.

Bachelard, Gaston. *La Philosophie du non. Essais d'une philosophie du nouvel esprit scientifique*. Paris: Presses Universitaires de France, 1981.

—. *La Poétique de l'espace*. Paris: Presses Universitaires de France, 1978.

Bakhtin, Mikhail. *The Dialogic Imagination*. Ed. Michael Holquist. Translated by Caryl Emerson and Michael Holquist. Austin: U of Texas P, 1981.

—. *Problems of Dostoevsky's Poetics*. Edited and Translated by Caryl Emerson. Introduction by Wayne C. Booth. Minneapolis: U of Minnesota P, 1984.

Barbachano Ponce, Miguel. *El diario de José Toledo*. México: Premiá, 1988.

Barthes, Roland. *La Chambre claire. Notes sur la photographie*. Paris: Gallimard Seuil, 1980.

—. *Le Degré zéro de l'écriture*. Paris: Editions du Seuil, 1972.

—. *Mythologies*. Paris: Editions du Seuil, 1957.

Bartra, Roger. Prólogo a *La sierra tarahumara o los desvelos de la modernidad en México,* de Juan Cajas Castro. México, D.F.: Consejo Nacional para la Cultura y las Artes, 1992.

Bataille, Georges. *L'Érotisme*. Paris: Les Editions de Minuit, 1992.

Baudrillard, Jean. *For a Critique of the Political Economy of the Sign*. Trans. and Introd. by Charles Levin. St. Louis, Mo.: Telos P, 1981.

Benjamin, Walter. *Illuminations*. Introd. and Ed. by Hannah Arendt. Trans. by Harry Zohn. New York: Schocken Books, 1969.

—. *Reflections. Essays, Aphorisms, Autobiographical Writings.* Introduced and Edited by Peter Demetz. New York: Schocken Books, 1989.

Bermúdez, Silvia. "Sexing the Bildungsroman: *Las edades de Lulú*, Pornography, and the Pleasure Principle." *Bodies and Biases: Sexualities in Hispanic Cultures and Literatures*. Ed. by David William Foster and Roberto Reis. Minneapolis: U of Minnesota P, 1996. 165–83.

Bernheimer, Charles, ed. *Comparative Literature in the Age of Multiculturalism*. Baltimore: Johns Hopkins UP, 1995.

Beverly, John. *Against Literature*. Minneapolis: U of Minnesota P, 1993.

—. "The Real Thing." *I, Rigoberta Menchú. Symposium at the University of Wisconsin Milwaukee*, March 25, 1994.

Bhabha, Homi K. "Of Mimicry and Man: The Ambivalence of Colonial Discourse." *October* 28 (Spring 1984): 125–33.

—. *The Politics of Location*. London: Routledge, 1994.

Blanchot, Maurice. *Lautréamont et Sade*. Paris: Les Editions de Minuit, 1963.

Blanco, José Joaquín. *Las púberes canéforas*. México, D.F.: Océano, 1987.

Borbolla, Oscar de la. *Todo está permitido*. México, D.F.: Planeta, 1994.

—. *Ucronías*. México, D.F.: Joaquín Mortiz, 1990.

Brooks, Peter. "Must We Apologize?" In *Comparative Literature in the Age of Multiculturalism*. Ed. Charles Bernheimer. Baltimore: Johns Hopkins UP, 1995. 97–106.

Brushwood, John.S. *México en su novela*. México, D.F.: Fondo de Cultura Económica, 1973.

Butler, Judith. *Gender Trouble. Feminism and the Subversion of Identity*. New York: Routledge, 1990.

—. *Bodies That Matter. On the Discursive Limits of Sex*. New York: Routledge, 1993.

Cajas Castro, Juan. *La sierra tarahumara o los desvelos de la modernidad en México*. México, D.F.: Consejo Nacional para la Cultura y las Artes,

1992.

Carrier, Joseph. *De los otros: Intimacy and Homosexuality among Mexican Men*. New York: Columbia UP, 1995.

Castillo, Debra. *Talking Back: Toward a Latin American Feminist Literary Criticism.* Ithaca: Cornell UP, 1992.

Chow, Rey. "In the Name of Comparative Literature." In *Comparative Literature in the Age of Multiculturalism*. Ed. Charles Bernheimer. Baltimore: Johns Hopkins UP, 1995. 107–16.

Cixous, Hélène. "Sorties: Out and Out: Attacks/Ways Out/Forays." *The Feminist Reader*. Edited by Catherine Belsey and Jane Moore. New York: Basil Blackwell, 1989. 101–16.

Cockcroft, James D. *Mexico. Class Formation, Capital Accumulation and the State*. New York: Monthly Review P, 1983.

Crouzet, Michel. *Stendhal et le langage*. Paris: Editions Gallimard, 1981.

Curry Holden, William. *Teresita*. Maryland: Owings Mills, 1978.

De Certeau, Michel. "Practices of Space." *On Signs*. Ed. Marshall Blonsky. Baltimore: The Johns Hopkins P, 1985. 122–45.

—. *The Writing of History*. Trans. by Tom Conley. New York: Columbia UP, 1988.

De Lauretis, Teresa. "Sexual Indifference and Lesbian Representation." *Theater Journal* 40 (1988): 155–77.

—. *Technologies of Gender: Essays on Theory, Film, and Fiction*. Bloomington: Indiana UP, 1987.

De Man, Paul. *The Rhetoric of Romanticism*. New York: Columbia UP, 1984.

Deleuze, Gilles, and Guattari, Félix. *A Thousand Plateaus: Capitalism and Schizophrenia*. Trans. and Foreword by Brian Massumi. Minneapolis: U of Minnesota P, 1988.

Derrida, Jacques. *Memoirs of a Blind: The Self-Portrait and Other Ruins*. Trans. by Pascale-Anne Brault and Michael Naas. Chicago: U of Chicago P, 1993

—. *Of Grammatology*. Trans. by Gayatri Chakravorty Spivak. Baltimore: The Johns Hopkins P, 1976.

Desnoes, Edmundo. "Cuba Made me So." *On Signs*. Ed. by Marshall Blonsky. Baltimore: The Johns Hopkins P, 1985. 384–403.

Didi-Huberman, Georges. *Invention de l'hystérie. Charcot et l'iconographie photographique de La Salpetrière*. Paris: Macula, 1983.

Diez Canedo, Joaquín. "Los editores en entrevista." *Vice versa* 3 (March-April 1993): 58-60.

Domecq, Brianda. *La insólita historia de la Santa de Cabora*. México, D.F.: Planeta, 1990.

Donato, Eugenio. "The Ruins of Memory: Archeological Fragments and Textual Artifacts." *MLN; Modern Language Notes* 93 (1978): 575–96.

Felman, Shoshana, and Doris Laub. *Testimony: Crises of Witnessing in Literature, Psychoanalysis, and History*. New York: Routledge, 1992.

Field, Trevor. *Form and Function in the Diary Novel*. London: MacMillan P, 1989.

Foster, David William. "The Case for Feminine Pornography in Latin America." *Bodies and Biases: Sexualities in Hispanic Cultures and Literatures*. Eds. David William Foster and Roberto Reis. Minneapolis: U of Minnesota P, 1996. 246–73.

—. *Gay and Lesbian Themes in Latin American Writing*. Austin: U of Texas P, 1991.

—. *Latin American Writers on Gay and Lesbian Themes. A Bio-Critical Sourcebook*. Westport, Conn.: Greenwood P, 1994.

Foucault, Michel. *Histoire de la folie à l'âge classique*. Paris: Editions Gallimard, 1972.

Francisco Torres, Vicente. "Novela mexicana: de la Onda a nuestros días." *Memoria de papel* 2:3 (April 1992): 132–42.

Franco, Jean. "Apuntes sobre la crítica feminista y la literatura hispanoamericana." *Hispamérica* 45 (1986): 31-43.

Franco, Jean. *Plotting Women: Gender and Representation in Mexico*. New York: Columbia UP, 1989.

Freud, Sigmund. *The Interpretation of Dreams*. New York: Avon Books, 1965.

Galindo, Carlos Blas. "Cultura artística y homosexualidad." *Ex profeso. Recuento de afinidades*. México, D.F.: Círculo Gay, 1990. 16–20.

Gandelman, Claude. *Le Regard dans le texte. Image et écriture du Quattrocento au XXe siècle*. Paris: Méridiens-Klincksieck, 1986.

Gates, Henri Louis, ed. *Race, Writing, and Difference*. Chicago: Chicago U P, 1985.

Geduldig, Lisa. "An Interview with Sara Levi Calderón." *Out Look: National Lesbian and Gay Quarterly* 13 (1991): 37–41.

Glantz, Margo. *La lengua en la mano*. México, D.F.: Premiá, 1983.

Godzich, Wlad. *The Culture of Literacy*. Cambridge: Harvard U P, 1994

González Rodríguez, Sergio. *Los amorosos. Relatos eróticos mexicanos*. México, D.F.: Cal y Arena, 1993.

—. *Los bajos fondos. El antro, la bohemia y el café*. México, D.F.: Cal y Arena,

1989.
—. "Lecturas prohibidas en México 1900–1930." *Inter Medios* 2 (June 1992): 30–39.
Goodwin, Sarah Webster. "Cross Fire and Collaboration among Comparative Literature, Feminism, and the New Historicism." In *Borderwork. Feminist Engagements with Comparative Literature*. Ed. Margaret R. Higonnet. Ithaca: Cornell U P, 1994. 247–66.
Griffin, Jasper. "The Love that Dared to Speak its Name." *The New York Review of Books* 39.17 (October 22, 1992): 30–33.
Halbwachs, Maurice. *La Mémoire collective*. Paris: Presses Universitaires de France, 1968.
Halperin, David M. *One Hundred Years of Homosexuality and Other Essays on Greek Love*. London: Routledge, 1990.
Hans, Marie-Françoise, and Lapouge Gilles. *Les Femmes, la pornographie, l'érotisme*. Paris: Editions du Seuil, 1978.
Heath, Stephen. "Male Feminism." *Men in Feminism*. Eds. Alice Jardine and Paul Smith. New York: Methuen, 1987.
Heidegger, Martin. *The Question Concerning Technology and Other Essays*. Trans. and Introd. by William Lovitt. New York: Harper Torchbooks, 1977.
Holden, William Curry. *Teresita*. Austin: U of Texas P, 1978.
Jameson, Frederic. *The Political Unconscious*. Ithaca: Cornell U P, 1981.
Johnson, Barbara. "Threshold of Difference: Stuctures of Address in Zora Neale Hurston." *Race, Writing, and Difference*. Ed. by Henri Louis Gates. Chicago: Chicago U P, 1985. 317–28.
—. *A World of Difference*. Baltimore: Johns Hopkins UP, 1988.
Kaplan, Caren. "Deterritorializations: The Rewriting of Home and Exile in Western Feminist Discourse." *Cultural Critique* 6 (1987): 187-98.
Knight, Alan. *The Mexican Revolution: Porfirians, Liberals and Peasants*. New York: Cambridge U P, 1986.
Koundoura, Maria. "Naming Gayatri Spivak." *Stanford Humanities Review* 1.1. (1989): 84–97.
Kristeva, Julia. *Revolution in Poetic Language*. Translated by Margaret Walk. New York: Columbia U P, 1984.
—. *Texto de la novela*. Trans. by Jordi Llovet. Barcelona: Lumen, 1981.
Kroker, Arthur, and David Cook. *The Postmodern Scene*. New York: Saint Martin P, 1986.
Lacan, Jacques. *The Four Fundamental Concepts of Psycho-Analysis*. Trans. by

Alan Sheridan. New York: Norton, 1981.

Lafaye, Jacques. "La Bonne Mère des mexicains." *Guadalupe: Epiphanie d'un métissage*. Paris: Le Centre Culturel du Mexique, 1989.

Lamas, Marta. "Freud y las muchachas: 20 años de feminismo." *El nuevo arte de amar. Usos y costumbres sexuales en México*. México, D.F.: Cal y Arena, 1990. 66–77.

Lanser, Susan Sniader. "Compared to What? Global Feminism, Comparatism, and the Master's Tolls." In *Borderwork. Feminist Engagements with Comparative Literature*. Ed. Margaret R. Higonnet. Ithaca: Cornell U P, 1994. 280–300.

Laplanche, J. and Pontalis, J-B. *The Language of Psychoanalysis*. Translated by Donald Nicholson-Smith. New York: W. W. Norton, 1973.

Larsen, Neil. *Reading North by South. On Latin American Literature, Culture, and Politics*. Minneapolis: U of Minnesota P, 1995.

Lau Jaiven, Ana. *La nueva ola del feminismo en México: Conciencia y acción de lucha de las mujeres*. México, D.F.: Planeta, 1987.

Lefebvre, Henri. *La Production de l'espace*. Paris: Editions Anthropos, 1974.

Lejeune, Philipe. "Le Pacte autobiographique bis." *Poétique* 56 (November 1983): 416–35.

Lumsden, Ian. *Homosexualidad, sociedad y el estado en México*. Trans. by Luis Zapata. México, D.F.: Solediciones, Colectivo Sol, 1991.

Martens, Lorna. *The Diary Novel*. New York: Cambridge U P, 1985.

Matthews, Tede. "Bienvenidos a Jotolandia." *Out Look. National Lesbian and Gay Quarterly* 15 (Winter 1992): 56–61.

Menchú, Rigoberta. *Me llamo Rigoberta Menchú y así me nació la conciencia*. Ed. Elizabeth Burgos. México, D.F.: Siglo Veintiuno, 1985.

Michelfelder, Diane, and Richard Palmer, eds. *Dialogue and Deconstruction: The Gadamer-Derrida Encounter*. New York: State U of New York P, 1989.

Molloy, Silvia. *At Face Value. Autobiographical Writing in Spanish America*. New York: Cambridge U P, 1991.

Monsiváis, Carlos. *Escenas de pudor y liviandad*. México, D.F.: Grijalbo, 1988.

—. "Las mitologías del cine mexicano." *Intermedios* 2 (June 1992): 6–12.

—. "Paisaje de batalla entre condones." *El nuevo arte de amar*. México, D.F.: Cal y Arena, 1990. 165–77.

—. Prefacio. Luis Morrett Alatorre, *La lucha por la tierra en los valles del Yaqui y mayo. Historia oral del sur de Sonora*. México, D.F.: Universidad Autónoma de Chapingo, 1989. 1–7.

Montalvo, Enrique. *El nacionalismo contra la nación*. México, D.F.: Grijalbo, 1985.

Morris, Meaghan. "Banality in Cultural Studies." *Logics of Television*. Ed. Patricia Mellencamp. Bloomington: Indiana U P, 1990. 14–43.

Nandino, Elías. *Erotismo al rojo blanco*. México, D.F.: Editorial Domés, 1982.

Nora, Pierre. "Entre Mémoire et histoire: la problématique des lieux." *La République*. Edition de Pierre Nora. Paris: Gallimard, 1984. xvii–xlii.

Parker, Andrew, Mary Russo, Doris Sommer, Patricia Yaeger, eds. *Nationalism and Sexualities*. New York: Routledge, 1992.

Paz, Octavio. *El laberinto de la soledad*. México, D.F.: Fondo de Cultura Económica, 1980.

—. *La llama doble. Amor y erotismo*. Barcelona: Seix Barral, 1994

Petro, Patrice. "After Shock/Between Boredom and History." *Fugitive Images. From Photography to Video*. Ed. Patrice Petro. Bloomington: Indiana U P, 1995. 265–84.

Poniatowska, Elena. *¡Ay vida no me mereces!* México, D.F.: Joaquín Mortiz, 1991.

Portal, Marta. *Proceso narrativo de la revolución mexicana*. Madrid: Espasa-Calpe, 1980.

Pratt, Mary Louise. *Imperial Eyes. Travel Writing and Transculturation*. London: Routledge, 1992

Ramos, Julio. *Desencuentros de la modernidad en América Latina. Literatura y política en el siglo XIX*. México, D.F.: Fondo de Cultura Económica, 1989.

Ramos, Samuel. *El perfil del hombre y de la cultura en México*. México, D.F.: Espasa-Calpe Mexicana, 1934.

Rice Pereira, Irene. *The Nature of Space*. Excerpts from *Voicing our Visions*. Ed. Mara R. Witzling. New York: Universe, 1991.

Robbe-Grillet, Alain. *Pour un nouveau roman*. Paris: Les Editions de Minuit, 1963.

Roffiel, Rosamaría. *Amora*. México, D.F.: Planeta, 1989.

Ronquillo, Víctor. "Editores en México: nace un libro." *Memoria de papel* 4:9 (March 1994): 4–20.

Rousset, Jean. *Forme et signification*. Paris: Editions Gallimard, 1969.

Rubin, Gayle. "Thinking Sex: Notes for a Radical Theory of the Politics of Sexuality." *Pleasure and Danger*. Ed. Carol S. Vance, New York: Routledge, 1984. 267–320.

Ruiz, Jorge Esparza. "Homotextualidad: la diferencia y la escritura." Coloquio

Internacional *Escritura y sexualidad en la literatura hispanoamericana*. Madrid: Fundamentos, 1990. 233–52.

Sarte, Jean Paul. *L'Imaginaire. Psychologie phénoménologique de l'imagination*. Paris: Gallimard, 1940.

Schaefer Rodríguez, Claudia. *Danger Zones: Homosexuality, National Identity, and Mexican Culture*. Tucson: U of Arizona P, 1996.

—. "The Power of Subversive Imagination: Homosexual Utopian Discourse in Contemporary Mexican Literature." *Latin American Literary Review* 33 (1989): 29–41.

—. *Testured Lives: Women, Art, and Representation in Modern Mexico*. Tucson: U of Arizona P, 1992.

Schneider, Luis Mario. "El tema homosexual en la nueva narrativa mexicana." *Casa del tiempo* 49–50 (1985): 82–86.

Sedgwick, Eve K. *Between Men: English Literature and Male Homosocial Desire*. New York: Columbia U P, 1985.

—. *Epistemology of the Closet*. Berkeley: U of California P, 1990.

Sefchovich, Sara. *Demasiado amor*. México, D.F.: Planeta, 1990.

—. *Mujeres en espejo*. México: Folios Ediciones, 1983.

Serres, Michel. "Les Anges sont de retour." Entretien avec Elisabeth Tingry. *Biba* 167 (January 1994): 92–93.

—. *Hermes: Literature, Science, Philosophy*. Ed. Josué V. Harari and David F. Bell. Baltimore: The Johns Hopkins P, 1981.

Silverman, Kaja. *Male Subjectivity at the Margins*. New York: Routledge, 1992.

—. "What is a Camera?, or: History in the Field of Vision." *Discourse* 15.3 (Spring 1993): 3–57.

Siméon, Rémi. *Diccionario de la lengua nahuatl o mexicana*. Trad. de Josefina Oliva de Coll. México, D.F.: Siglo XXI, 1977.

Sklodowska, Elzbieta. "Wor(l)ds in Dispute: Afterthoughts on Testimonio and Rigoberta Menchú." *I, Rigoberta Menchú. Symposium at the University of Wisconsin Milwaukee*, March 25, 1994.

Smith, Paul Julian. *The Body Hispanic: Gender and Sexuality in Spanish and Spanish American Literature*. Oxford: Clarendon P, 1989.

Sommer, Doris. "Sin secretos." *Revista de crítica literaria latinoamericana* 18:36 (1992): 135–53.

Sullivan, Edward. *Aspects of Contemporary Mexican Painting*. New York: Americas Society, 1990.

Taussig, Michael. *Shamanism, Colonialism, and the Wild Man*. Chicago: The U P of Chicago, 1987.

Torgovnick, Marianna. *Gone Primitive. Savage Intellects, Modern Lives*. Chicago: U Chicago P, 1990.

Torres, Vicente F. "De la Onda a nuestros días." *Memoria de papel* 2:3 (April 1992): 132–42.

Trejo Fuentes, Ignacio. "Al filo de una apuesta." *Memoria de papel* 2:3 (April 1992): 142–47

Valis, Noël. "Adorning Women: The Feminine as *Cursi*." Unpublished manuscript.

Vidal, Hernán, ed. *Cultural and Historical Grounding for Hispanic and Luzo-Brazilian Feminist Literary Criticism*. Minneapolis: Institute for the Study of Ideologies and Literature, 1989.

Williams, Linda. *Hard Core. Power, Pleasure and the Frenzy of the Visible.* Berkeley: U of California P, 1989.

Wolin, Judith. "The Rhetorical Question." *Vía: Journal of the Graduate School of Fine Arts at the University of Pennsylvania* 8 (1986): 18–35.

Zapata, Luis. *Las aventuras, desventuras y sueños de Adonis García, el vampiro de la Colonia Roma*. México, D.F.: Editorial Grijalbo, 1979.

Zea, Leopoldo. *Apogeo y decadencia del positivismo en México*. México, D.F.: Fondo de Cultura Económica, 1944.

INDEX